LORDS OF THE MOUNTAINS

SOUTHERN PERSIA &
THE KASHKAI TRIBE

Malek Mansur's Falconer

LORDS OF
THE MOUNTAINS

Southern Persia and the Kashkai Tribe

BY

MARIE-THÉRÈSE
ULLENS de SCHOOTEN

1956
CHATTO & WINDUS
LONDON

PUBLISHED BY
CHATTO AND WINDUS LTD
42 WILLIAM IV STREET
LONDON WC2

★

CLARKE, IRWIN AND CO LTD
TORONTO

PRINTED IN GREAT BRITAIN BY
ROBERT CUNNINGHAM AND SONS LTD
LONGBANK WORKS, ALVA

I am never alone
For had we not decided
To travel these roads together? . . .

Some day
In the noon heat and sun
The valley bells will toll
And we shall meet again!

TO JEAN, MY HUSBAND, IN LOVING MEMORY

And to those who on a lonely trail
Fear neither shadows nor darkness
But who through life have kept their smile
Their courage . . .
And have opened their hearts
To other peoples' sorrows.

TO ANDRÉ AND YEDDA GODARD

AND TO BIBI KHANUM, 'THE LADY'

FOREWORD

(ACKNOWLEDGEMENTS)

TWO white figures stood guard over the years of my childhood and youth. Silvery hair framing her exquisitely chiselled features, my beloved English governess hovered attentively over me, patiently teaching me her language, guiding me from the first stumbling syllables to the delights of nursery rhymes and fairy tales. Later, in this now distant though not dim past, clad in immaculate flowing robes, a teacher took me through the intricacies of English literature and poetry, and introduced me to the delights of discovering not only the history of works of art and of the great Masters of the past, but, scattered over the earth, their presence in Museums and Collections. To them go my grateful thoughts for having started me on a road filled with oft renewed wonder and surprise.

When, in 1931, I watched Ella Maillart, then Captain of the Swiss Ladies' Team, ski down the Mürren slopes, little could I guess that her subsequent wanderings and journeys would influence my life. Sixteen years later, browsing in a London book-store, I came upon her *Cruel Way*. Together, my husband and I, looking at some of the striking photographs that illustrated it, decided then and there to visit Persia. To Ella go my thanks, as also to my husband's friend and colleague, then Belgian Minister in Iran, and to his wife, Comte and Comtesse de Laubespin, who welcomed us there.

And to many others I am grateful. To a friend of my childhood, Lady Kelly, met again after many years of absence, whose initiative and advice launched this manuscript on its career. To Ronald Armstrong, M. A. Jamalzade, Lawrence Lockhart, and Professors Henri Massé and Vladimir Minorsky, for their valuable help and knowledge. To Jean Lartéguy who, with friendly unselfishness handed to me all the information he had carefully gathered about the tribes. To my mother and my children who excuse and forgive my wanderlust and patiently await my return.

To the regretted René Grousset who encouraged me on this venture.

But first and foremost they are due to André and Yedda Godard, who taught me all I know about Persia and its art; and to the Kashkai for their hospitality and to Molki Bayat-Kashkai in particular for the information she gave me on their customs and habits.

Paradoxically, I believe I should also have a certain amount of amused and slightly ironical gratitude for those whose friendship became strangely aloof, and whose reticence or scepticism were a very challenge, their silence daring me to attempt a difficult task and spurring me on this hazardous path.

CONTENTS

COLOUR PLATES

10

MONOCHROME PLATES

INTRODUCTION

MY childhood was fed on oriental tales. One of my uncles lived in China. When he came back on leave, at very distant intervals, he and his wife would tell us in their charming and delicate manner stories of a country where, to my young mind, everything seemed to be the colour of gold: the varnished crest-tiles of the roofs; the gleam of shimmering silks.

Later, I lived in a haze that was the colour of the sky. Seeing that I had learnt to read, another uncle gave me a beautiful volume bound in turquoise leather, illustrated by many lovely pictures. For the first time, my imagination was carried to a land of poetry and legend. It has never quite returned.

My husband was a diplomat. Our life was spent on four continents. I have seen the largest ports and docks, visited the most imposing factories, the biggest and noisiest cities. But I have always preferred the solitude of high mountain or deep forest, the mystery of a nordic saga.

We had often skirted the borders of Iran and for a long time had lived in Egypt. With Howard Carter we had walked down into Tutankhamen's tomb and counted and studied its treasures. Hasanein Bey, the explorer, had taught us to love the desert. Lord Lloyd would tell us of his adventures with Lawrence, while Gertrude Bell's letters had incited us to journey to Iraq with the sole purpose of visiting the Museum to which she eventually dedicated her life.

My dream persisted, in spite of our wandering life, the horrors of wars, the uncertain plans and journeys.

The ancient name of Persia, with its implications of history and art, sounded in our ears. We wanted to travel there and devoted an entire holiday to this purpose. Immediately, a spell was cast!

Beyond the years, and sadness, and bereavement, the dream remained everlasting.

Three times more I journeyed there.

Photo: Yedda Godard

On the trail

YEDDA'S THREE LETTERS

1950

I AM writing to you from the terrace of Persepolis, in the stillness and silence of the desert, and the serene, fading light of an ending day.

There are times when words fail or are inadequate, and when even friendship and sympathy are at a loss.

But the beauty of the world is unchanging.

The solitary grandeur of the Persian horizon; the powerful winds blowing over the Asian highlands; the great ruins of the past may be a solace and a new inspiration.

Come out and work!

1951

YOU have now seen the most noble historical remains, the splendid landscapes of Demavend and Elburz, the shores of the Caspian Sea.

What you should see in a land where tradition ordains even the gesture of the humble ploughman, is the spectacle that, for thousands of years, has renewed itself each spring: the migration of entire tribes moving slowly, solemnly, from pasture-ground to pasture-ground, according to ancient rules and changeless customs.

1952

SOON after the war I travelled to Shiraz and, one morning, visited the 'Bagh-è-Aram' the estate belonging to the Kashkai Chiefs. They had been deprived of it during the reign of Riza Shah Pahlevi. Freed from their prison and exile by this sovereign's abdication in 1941, they had hurried back to their Tribes and had taken over, once more, this long-abandoned garden.

It was therefore well tended and more beautiful than I had ever known it to be.

The attentive house-steward sent me tea, then came to tell me that 'Madam was at home'.

Fearing some futile conversation, I left with regret the shade of the tall cypresses that form a solid wall, and came forward, deciding to cut this visit short.

I saw a lady clothed according to ancient fashion: her hair covered by a white veil, long and flowing skirts. Her eyes were vivacious, her features fine, and her demeanour stately.

I did not know who she was. The sentence used by the servant: 'Khanum Buzurg Injast' made me believe that she might be the mistress of this estate. We chatted in Persian, and I complimented her on her garden: 'You must be happy to live here?'

'No', she answered, 'I prefer living under tents. I love above all to travel on horseback and to camp near a spring where the sound of running water soothes the heart. I love the nomadic life during migration, the journey to the summer camps amongst our people. It is a joy I have long been deprived of and fully appreciate.'

Her enthusiasm, her sincerity in expressing feelings that many now consider out of date, astonished and enchanted me. This spirit of decision, this courage, this valour, aroused my sympathy.

Having bade her farewell, I enquired:

'Who is she?'

And was told:

'She is called BIBI KHANUM, "the Lady".'

Photo: Yedda Godard

PLATE I   The Kashkai migrating (This photograph decided
the author to journey to Southern Persia)   (Page 15)

PLATE 2.   'The solitary grandeur of the Persian horizon'
(Page 15)

Part I

PRELUDE TO THE SOUTH

B

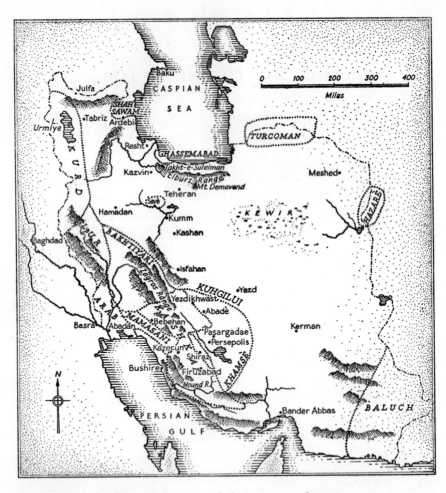

The approximate tribal territories of Persia

MY FRIENDS ANDRÉ
AND YEDDA GODARD

LEAVING Paris we had been told: 'You must meet the Godards. He is General Director of the Archaeological Services of Iran. They have lived in Iran for over twenty years; their love and understanding of the country, their knowledge of its art and history are unsurpassed.'

I shall always remember Yedda as I saw her, in 1948, for the first time, walking down the main gallery of the Museum, her silvery hair blowing halo-wise about her face in the draught. She was carrying carefully one of the most precious and exquisite Islamic vases that was being packed off to the Paris exhibition. The ring on her finger matched its perfect shade of turquoise. I was immediately struck by the kind look she gave me and, through two or three short sentences, by her devastating and irresistible sense of humour. A painter, a student of Arabic and Persian, an unquestioned authority on miniatures, totally indifferent to things material, delightfully absent-minded, she has nevertheless, I realised, during our various expeditions, brought to perfection the knack of travelling light. What matter if a room is drab? A lovely, ancient 'Kalamkar' will spread its folds on the rickety table; its colours will make one forget that the walls are dingy and covered with stains. A silver bowl, ashtray for her countless cigarettes, catches the light and the disappointed glance is arrested: the roving eye dwells on its intricate pattern and engraving. In the midday haze the desert is bleak and hostile? A rug of brilliant hues is rolled out, the picnic unpacked, and a few drops of cream and a dash of brandy soon give to the scraggy chicken, bought by the way-side, the flavour of the most parisian dish. For Yedda had also carried to Teheran the delights of French 'cuisine'; her recipes are famous, and scattered around the town, there are cooks proud to let it be known that they have worked for her. Arriving in distant Shiraz, the steward whispered that Abbas hearing of her visit, would serve her a feast. Alas, he seemed to have forgotten much of his vaunted knowledge, and the meal was rather dismal.

Silent, shy, immersed in the study of intellectual and archaeological problems, exacting in his pursuit of accuracy and perfection,
André Godard is constantly lost in deep thought. When he descends
from his clouds, sometimes brought back to earth by our peals of
laughter, he adds his dry wit and gentle sarcasm to Yedda's comments.
His high forehead is that of the thinker, the scholar. His trim neat
figure gives him the appearance of a high-ranking, Anglo-Saxon
officer. Swift and nimble-footed, he never shirks climbing to the
roof-top of any building, or of ascending the countless steep steps
of dome or minaret. A man of few words, his comments are always
to the point, the result of thoughtfully-weighed conclusions. His
clear grey-blue eyes have the candour of a trusting youth who believes in the beauty of the world and the noble aims of mankind,
though their amused twinkle proves that he sometimes has his
doubts. . .

They make a wonderful team.

Great patriots, fervent exponents of French culture, they have
both dedicated their life to art and history, to the Museum they have
planned and created, and to the admirable monuments that they
have often saved from neglect, and have tended with loving, selfless
devotion. Prehistoric and historic treasures are now assembled in
the Teheran sanctuary. Proud stone carvings gleam under their careful touch. Blue tiles shine again on once crumbling walls and
cupolas. . .

It is to be hoped that those who are proud of their artistic heritage,
and, those the world over, who are lovers of old masterpieces, of
works of art, will remember and be thankful for so great a service
rendered!

TEHERAN

THIS time, in Teheran, there had been little to do. The citizens were nervous, and officials sometimes went into careful and prudent retreat. Those who held the keys of the Imperial Library could not be traced, so this sanctuary was barred to us.

The Gulistan palace, surrounded by charming gardens, is in the centre of the modern town. Some of its halls and apartments are still used for state occasions and official functions; the others are the imperial museum.

I recalled other times when, in the quiet seclusion of the Gulistan Imperial Library, Yedda, who was studying some unknown manuscripts, would patiently explain to me the history, the perfection and the beauty of the intricate miniatures. Some, oddly enough, contained among their pages illustrations of European religious scenes, placed there and pasted onto the pages, centuries ago, by admiring Oriental princes. Others still bore the pencil marks and scratches of royal children whose picture-books they must have been.

Years ago I had been officially taken to see the famed 'Treasure of the Shah', brought back in triumph by Nadir Shah from the siege of Delhi, and the celebrated 'Peacock Throne'. Though impressed by the size and glitter of so many jewels, I could not admire this barbaric accumulation of wealth and splendour, this display of fabulous stones, attracted as I am by the beauty of simple lines, of solitary places, and of barren landscapes.

I preferred the peaceful hours spent in the Teheran Museum. This modern building was designed by André Godard: inspired by Sasanian architecture, he followed its tradition; the entrance is under a lofty arch, and the simplicity of the well-lit and unadorned halls sets off countless treasures. In the quiet, studious atmosphere, the prehistoric vases and the bold free drawings of the Nishapur ceramics of the tenth and the eleventh centuries, had for me a fascinating charm. Years ago, I had discovered a new world, when spending hours alone in the modest Baghdad Museum. Having read and re-read Gertrude Bell's Letters about its difficult start, it was with deep emotion that I contemplated these early potteries, so fragile and naïve and yet so perfect. So, in Teheran, it was always with a feeling of reverence and gratitude that I forsook the dusty street and the glare and heat of the sun, to wander under the arched vault and enter the calm and cool precincts of study.

Often, during the siesta hours, the door-bell would ring and Ali, the servant, would come and tell us that Soleiman, Jacoub or some other chap wished to be admitted to the Godard's home.

Shabbily clad, without collar or tie, they would be ushered in carrying a bundle and a dilapidated suitcase.

Though they differed in appearance, they all seemed to have the same plaintive, whining voice, the same expressive, gesticulating hands.

First they showered a litany of blessings upon us, then, with infinite care and, at the same time, with apparent abandon, they started unpacking their goods. As if they had never seen us before they repeated, time after time, the same rigmarole showing us, to begin with, nondescript bits of antiques, fragments of pottery, impudent, flagrant copies. Yedda would, in her brusque and frank manner, quickly tell them off and send them running. Then, from the depth of a dirty pocket they would sometimes, as if it cost them pain and sorrow, produce, wrapped in a rag or a filthy scrap of paper, an object of real beauty that would strike our fancy.

And then the fun and art of bargaining would begin in real earnest. Sometimes we would win, or at least think – for they are wily and clever – we had driven a good bargain. At others, we would have to be patient and hope that they might be tempted to turn up again; and sometimes, too, we would meet disappointment. . . I shall long remember the delightful twelfth-century glass bottle, coveted in the morning, and seen again that same afternoon among one of my friends' treasures! . . .

Then, too, there was the fun of exploring the recesses of the real antique-dealers' homes, of being shown as a great privilege a wonder-

ful example of Achaemenian art or a translucent fragment of Sasanian
carved glass. These, though they were stored in the oddest places – and
I have seen them brought out of cupboards where broken plates,
scraps of food and an old hat were thrown – were far beyond my
hopes and means, and would find their way, sooner or later, to some
private collection or to the showcase of some museum. But the thrill
of seeing them, of touching them, was nearly as great, for possession
is ephemeral and memory everlasting!

Carpet-dealers were among my friends. . . I would walk through
their shop and sit with them in their store-room, quietly sipping
glasses of very sweet tea, in an atmosphere thickened by dust that
increased every minute as rug after rug was unrolled for my in-
spection. It was not the fun of buying: for many years ago I had
done the same, sitting in a very famous Cairo shop where an aged,
cantankerous, but handsome and friendly and very celebrated dealer
had patiently pointed out to us the qualities, the various patterns of the persian rugs. These names, that have always set me
dreaming, had already become familiar to me in Cairo: Kerman . . .
Ardebil . . . Tabriz . . . Heriz . . . Bijar. Now I was in the country
itself, and it was a joy to behold once more this blaze of colour,
these geometrical or flowery designs, and to become acquainted
with the less known but bold and decorative tribal rugs, which
adorn a chief's tent, and are carried around the hills on the back of
a camel.

Only those who have wandered across the burning desert, through
'this ocean of incandescent light that covers the "Kéwir" ', or have
ridden over the barren mountains, will understand the charm of
secluded, walled-in gardens, the blessing of shade under 'chenar' or
palm-tree, the delight of the fountain's suggestive melody of freshness. . .

We had crossed a high mountain pass; the road twisted and turned
its way through a deep valley before climbing another steep ridge.
Eventually we discovered our friend's retreat, hidden in the Elburz
range. The door in the mud-wall was open. Sheltered alike from
wind and dust, we walked into peace and harmony. Though the
month was May, because of the altitude the trees were still bare and

the poplars' silvery trunks swayed above the wall to the eternal mountain breeze.

Beside the pool my friend greeted us. I thanked him for his hospitality, and while we were enjoying the 'pilaw' and 'kebab' he had prepared in this perfect setting, he told me the following tale:

'My father, who was a court official, loved this distant and remote spot. He planted this garden, built the pool and, enjoying it, wished to share it with all. He called to me one day: "My son, when I shall depart from this world, this garden that I cherished will be yours. But on one condition only. You must promise me to let all who pass this road enjoy its beauty, and rest in its shade." So now, see for yourself: years have passed, the wooden door has warped and can no longer close; its hinges have rusted away!' I looked up: In the doorway stood a pilgrim, a 'derwish', holding his stick and begging-bowl. He salamed deeply and, as if certain of his welcome, crossed the threshold and came and sat by our side.

I thought of our own parks and gardens, of high gates and entrance-fees, and marvelled at this unaffected hospitality. Could there be, for the tired passer-by, a more graceful gift than a few moments' rest in lovely surroundings?

This same friend, on another occasion, knowing of my interest and curiosity for things Persian, said to me: 'I am a Sufi and have a great devotion for our master, Pir Safi-Ali-Shah, who was a saint. Would you photograph his tomb?'

We drove from the noisy traffic-filled avenues to a side-street and knocked on a door. It was soon opened and we were admitted to another garden, astonishingly quiet in the midst of the turmoil and bustle of the city. I was an unbeliever and a woman; my presence was undoubtedly unwelcome; yet I was bade enter and asked to sit on the terrace of the 'Khanègah' among philosophers and ascetics. Nothing in their attire marked them as holy men, though all were adherents of a doctrine whose beliefs and high aspirations, diverging from strict Mohammedanism, are perhaps the result of a kind of escapism, of passive resistance to a religion enforced by the Arab conquest, and to which the Iranians amongst others have had to submit for centuries.

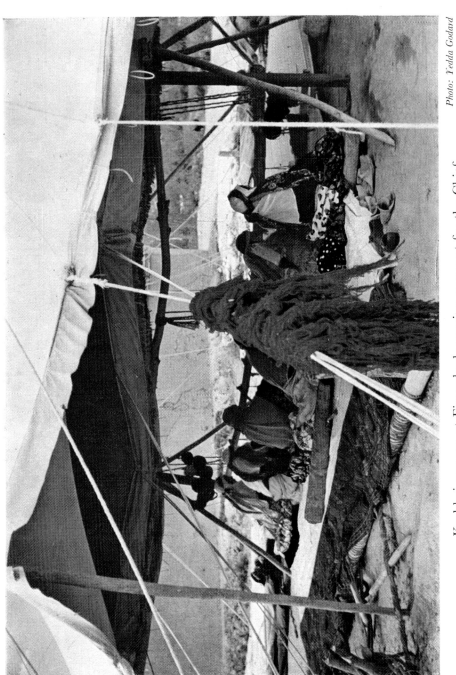

Kashkai women at Firuzabad weaving a carpet for the Chief

Fording the river at Tang-è-Ab

I had heard many mysterious stories and theories about them and it was strange to be in their midst. Shoes removed, we squatted on rugs spread on the terrace overhanging the pool. The Sufi chatted among themselves while I looked on, marvelling at Oriental ease and simplicity. I knew my host to be a court dignitary; here he was, engrossed in metaphysical discussion with a lorry driver whom I had seen stepping down from his truck!

Tea was prepared and I watched the elegant movement of hands and fingers: a few drops of water were poured into each glass, the contents spilled into the saucer; swiftly and deftly the glass was turned over and over on its side, in the saucer, to ensure its perfect cleanliness. Then only was the tea served. We sat on for awhile, enjoying the fragrance of our drink, then, with reverence, I was shown the tomb, and piously I set to work.

We did not forsake this religious, spiritual atmosphere: a few moments later we were to witness another, and very different, manifestation of its pervading influence.

From the now darkened street and still darker passage, we plunged into a well-lit, dome covered hall, and noise and smells met us as we walked in.

The 'Zur Khanè' (the 'house of strength') is a very ancient institution. Firdawsi (*circa* A.D. 1000) mentions it and the adepts of this kind of club perform to the sound of his historical poems, the verses of the 'Shah-Namè'.

Near the entrance, squatting in a recess, the drum-beater was at work, hitting, according to the changing rhythms, the big drum or the smaller, barrel-shaped instruments that he handled with amazing dexterity and skill, chanting all the while as he played.

Beside him a young boy sat looking on, swaying as if haunted and possessed by the music.

Spectators all around watched while men and boys in turn, stripped to the waist, walked into a circular arena in the centre of the hall and started their various movements that are not only physical exercises but have a heroic significance and a mystical discipline. As soon as they had limbered up they picked up clubs, and, swinging them to the beat of the drums, threw them high, catching them again before they reached the ground. Some of these gymnasts were slim, elegantly built youths, others were already ageing men. Was it this particular form of sport? As they grew older their shape changed sometimes strangely: their legs, thighs and hips remained slender, whereas their chests, arms and shoulders developed out of proportion.

We sat and watched, listening to the fascinating chant of heroic and ancient tales, drinking tea to the smell of sweating humanity, while one after another the performers, their exercises over, walked from the ring, and wrapped themselves in the typical red-checkered Iranian bath-towels. These hand-woven cloths are a familiar sight in towns and villages: put out to hang above the 'hammam's' roof they flutter in the breeze, indicating to the passer-by that on this day this particular bath is open and ready to welcome its patrons.

I looked at the drum-beater once more: the scene was changing. His young son was taking his place; small hands now beat out the rhythm and his shrill piercing voice filled the hall with the weird, antique music.

The last gymnast entered the arena and with incredible vigour and power swung the clubs and tossed them higher and higher till they reached the top of the dome. They were of great weight and would certainly have crushed or maimed him had they fallen on him from such a height. But though he was no longer young, his accuracy never failed him, and he caught them time and time again, balancing them at arms' length, and tossing them high once more, to the applause of admiring comrades and the sounding of the drums.

This throbbing, pulsating beat, haunted me for years. When I needed incidental music for my films, obliging friends set forth in search of local talent. Theirs was not a very easy task: radio now plays an important part in bazaar and 'chai-khanè' and foreign melodies insidiously insinuate themselves and weave their notes into the oriental pattern. It is now considered smart to 'harmonise' and 'occidentalise', and the old traditional tunes are played to a jazzy tempo. I would have nothing of this; we first recorded some stanzas of the 'Shah-Namè' and eventually humble artists were found and brought to me straight from their villages or valleys.

These were trying yet unforgettable hours: in a garden beside a tank the players in succession rehearsed their stock of folk melodies. Some were pleasing, others monotonous or strident to our untrained ears. I shall always see before me the sad face of a blind flute player who, bewitched and intoxicated by the sound of his own music, could not be made to stop. He did not know what we wanted nor why he was playing for us, but went on and on like a crazed nightingale till breath eventually failed him. The recorder was then switched on; suddenly, without warning, he was listening to his own music. . . Though his eyes remained closed, his expression changed, lost its sadness; bewilderment and unbelief took its place; then pure, unspoilt joy shone and radiated from his blind countenance.

ISFAHAN

'HOW did you get back so soon?' –
–'I took a taxi!'

This was my fourth visit to Isfahan.

We had planned to spend there several days of the Spring holiday. The Persian New Year, the 'Nauruz', which coincides with our first day of Spring had just been celebrated with all its gracious and charming customs born of centuries of tradition: visits to relatives, and the endless sampling and munching of sweetmeats, prepared especially for the occasion; exchange of greetings, of small presents; offerings of bowls of goldfish, of plants grown for these days, of pots of young wheat, their green, tender shoots a promise of the harvest to come.

For Persians the New Year coincides with the first day of Spring . . . a wonderful feeling!

The subsequent days are spent in festive mood. The bazaars are closed and the people roam the countryside. Carpets and rugs are spread in the fields. Seated on them, the women, in their bright new 'chador', are flower-like in the vast landscape. Water bubbles and boils in the samovars; tea is served constantly, and young and old alike enjoy the ceaseless picnic.

Isfahan, the glorious city, has grown on the banks of the 'Zendè-Rud', the 'River of Life'. In autumn a mere trickle of water on a bed of pebbles and stones, this rainy year it was a swift, deep stream. Ancient bridges, of a very particular architecture, span it at various points.

The previous days had been spent studying in Isfahan. The town contains, in their most perfect form, monuments of every type and period of Iranian Islamic art, and it is always a keen joy and a deep intellectual and religious experience to wander in this city.

At first perhaps, having read so many enthusiastic descriptions from ancient travellers, one is bound to be somewhat disappointed. . .

Seen from the air, the oasis, vast and flat amid jagged mountains, is dotted here and there with massive towers, built of brick, that give it the appearance of a well-defended fortress, but are, in reality, peaceful pigeon-lofts. Pigeon-breeding is undertaken on a large scale: the birds themselves are the principal menace to the old historical buildings around which they circle endlessly, their claws loosening the precious blue tiles as they alight on the cupolas. Their droppings, the rich fertiliser of the famous melon-fields, are the main source of plentiful crops.

The town itself, the second largest in Iran, is now the most industrialised, although, thanks to careful planning, its numerous factories are partially hidden among walled gardens.

As every traveller knows, Isfahan is one of the oldest cities of the world. Did not Nebuchadnezzar settle part of the Tribes of Israel on the banks of the 'Zendè-Rud', and was it not called 'Yahudiyè' – though it was also known as 'Jayy'? The site itself, a few miles south-east of the present city, is abandoned, and only large mounds of earth stand out in the ploughed fields, but the descendants of those tribes, of pure Jewish stock and type, still live on one side of the town.

Two thousand years later, other people were settled there by the will of Shah Abbas, who brought Armenians down from the north. These thrifty folk established themselves on the southern side of the river, gave the district the name of their former town 'Julfa', and built themselves palaces, churches and an entire city.

And to Shah Abbas goes the glory of Isfahan. He made this city his capital, and planned its large avenues, its wonderful gardens, the well proportioned and majestic Royal Place, the 'Maidan'.

Two seventeenth-century travellers, Pietro della Valle and the Chevalier Chardin, who lived there for many years, alternately give us this eye-witness description: 'In 1598 Shah Abbas laid out and planted the Chahar Bagh that joined his palace to his country gardens ... the Prince took such pleasure in having this beautiful avenue made that he desired that each tree be planted in his presence.' From the terrace of the palace gate, in itself a small palace called Ala Kapi, he could attend the processions of foreign envoys and ambassadors, the pageant of lumbering elephants, of elegant horses, or watch the game of polo being played by brilliant horsemen: 'The great portal opens on to the Royal Place. It is called Ala Kapi, which means the high gate or the sacred door ... the threshold is of porphyry of a green colour . . . the Persians hold it in reverence, as sacred, and those who walk on it have to be punished; it must be stepped over. Those who have received some favour from the King go and kiss it in pomp and ceremony, and, dismounting and standing erect, they pray out loud to God for the prince's prosperity. Out of respect the King never crosses it on horseback. . .' 'The hall prepared for holding audiences was that beautiful and spacious room built over the palace portal, and is the most lovely hall of its kind I have ever seen in the world. It is so high that looking down onto the place, men seem only two feet tall . . . the King and all his court numbering about three hundred having entered at nine o'clock, one saw, coming into the place from the eastern side the Lesqui (Daghestan) ambassador. The one from Muscovy appeared a quarter of an hour later and came from the same side. The Basra envoy followed. The gifts of these ambassadors were however at the end of the place, near the royal mosque. Pious people say that in bringing gifts from the east and from in front of the mosque one wants to prove that God is the origin and the giver of all things temporal, and that all the good things that happen to men are a gift of God. As soon as the presents were carried forth, drums, trumpets, and other instruments were played. . . This was the signal for games and fights and at the same moment the wrestlers, gladiators and fencers started with one another. The keepers of fierce beasts turned them loose onto young bulls that were held nearby, and those in charge of goats and young bulls trained to fight set them against each other. . . The spectacle of these different kinds of encounters lasted till eleven o'clock. Those that followed were more entertaining and natural. The first was of about three hundred riders that appeared from the four corners of the place, very well mounted and clothed as richly and elegantly as possible. They were for the most young lords of the court and all had several saddle-horses. For one hour they practised the game of mall* on horseback.' 'One reaches the private apartments by a narrow staircase . . . several stories consisting each of a small central hall surrounded by several small rooms. Towards the Maidan and on the opposite side are balconies according to their fashion, where they sit on the wooden floor and watch what is going on below. There are so many apartments and so many rooms with numerous

* Polo.

passages that the doorkeepers say there must be five hundred in the house, though small like all the rest. The beauty of this house resides in its walls enriched with gold from top to bottom, with excellent miniatures in different colours. . .' 'One of the marvels of the town is the Maidan, or main place that is in front of the Royal Palace. It is of a length of about six hundred and eighty of my paces and wide of about two hundred and thirty. It is decorated all around by great portals of the most beautiful and regular symmetry one can describe, uninterrupted by any street or by anything else. These portals, on which one has built balconies with big casements and a thousand small and very agreeable ornaments, are as many shops filled with various merchandise.'

To Shah Abbas, too, goes the glory of the Royal Mosque (Masjid-è-Shah) which remains standing as a tribute to his memory, a perfect work of art.

He wished it and willed it, and had it built in a hurry. The architect, knowing the risk of moving sands and faulty foundations, refused to go on with the work. Angered, the Shah ordered him to be beheaded, so the poor man went into hiding. Years passed, the foundations settled, the wise architect reappeared, proved his point, and was forgiven. And to him we owe this unique monument.

The patterns in the more ancient mosques were made of patiently and artistically assorted fragments of enamelled pottery known as 'Kashi', worked into beautiful mosaics, the recurring theme found first in woven carpets: the design of a Persian garden and its lovely flowers. To Shah Abbas, time meant apparently a lot. He wanted to see his mosque completed, perfect; so the work was simplified. The painstaking, careful and elaborate mosaics were replaced by large slabs of painted and enamelled earthenware. The fineness and delicacy are somewhat lost, but the effect of all these varied colours, ranging from deep lapis-lazuli to the palest shades of turquoise blue, enhanced by splashes of vivid yellow and heightened and set off by an alabaster wainscoting, is powerful and entrancing.

As the sun sets, its rays slant through the arches of the courtyard; the edges of the large flagstones catch the light and stand out in irregular pattern, the quiet pool reflects the depth and the mystery, the misty blue of the darkened 'Iwan'.

The town has changed; the palaces have disappeared, the gardens of the Chahar Bagh have been replaced by booths or shops; but, in the quiet of Chehel Sutun, the Palace of the Forty Columns whose twenty slender cedar shafts are reflected in the clear pond, or in the courtyards of the various mosques, the charm and majesty of vanished days can be recaptured.

At early dawn or in the twilight, we would walk through the side streets and catch glimpses of quiet and charming gardens hidden by high walls, and, crossing the threshold of lofty gates, would enter one or another mosque.

The keeper, knowing us well, would smile at us and let us wander on our solitary way. Often, by dark passages and steep stairs, we climbed onto the roof and, standing in the shadow of some majestic cupola, looked down upon the town.

From below, surging against the walls, reverberating in the dome, the sound of prayer would be wafted on the air: the beautiful call to God, the chanting of Allah's ninety-nine names, or a funeral dirge in honour of one of the martyred 'Imam', would echo all around us, recalling vividly the eternity of Spirit and the everlasting Presence.

Who cared then for the bustle of the streets, the excitement of political conflict, the impudence of agitated youths?

Time ceased to count. . .

And then my camera jammed . . . and from my lofty view-point, far above the city, I was disagreeably and suddenly brought down to earth! Here I was, stranded in Isfahan, with reels and reels of film, a definite goal, and a cantankerous camera.

I spent a dismal evening, full of forebodings, and next morning, with the patient help of André, took the camera to pieces. But I am no mechanic, and nail scissors and a file are rather inadequate instruments! Outwardly calm and cool, I hope, by midday I was frantic. A quick decision was needed, for two days later the Spring Festival would take place and, after that, all our trip to the South would be in jeopardy. The plane was due to leave in a few minutes, I hopped aboard, and though the weather was bad, and the clouds hanging low on the jagged mountains, we skidded and zigzagged in and out of them and wound our way back to Teheran.

Here my luck held and, by nightfall, a charming and unknown gentleman was coaxed into lending me his own camera; meanwhile,

PLATE 3

'The Bagh-è-Aram',
e 'Garden of Heaven',
the Kashkai home
in Shiraz
(Page 15)

André Godard,
Director General of
the Archaeological
Services of Iran

Photo: Yedda Godard

'Her silvery hair
blowing halo-wise
about her face'
Yedda Godard,
André Godard's wife
(Page 19)

PLATE 5. 'As the sun sets, its rays slant through the arches of the courtyard.' Masjid-è-Shah, the Royal Mosque, at Isfahan (Page 31)

PLATE 6   'Crossing the threshold of lofty gates'
Entrance to the Masjid-è-Jum'a, the Friday Mosque, Isfahan (Page 32)

he would repair mine. Really, the courtesy and hospitality of the East is sometimes boundless!

So now, back to Isfahan. . .

The morning light was bleak on the airfield. Huge clouds loomed up on the horizon and the pilot refused to take off. 'Could I still catch a bus?' – 'Yes, of course.' Back to Teheran in a frenzy of haste. – 'The bus?' – 'Oh, it left hours ago!' – 'The next?' – 'To-morrow, or some other day . . . they seem all booked up.' Somebody, ironically, suggested a taxi. After all, why not? Fortune smiles on those who dare. I wanted those pictures, did I not? Why hesitate?

We made it in record time, flying over the bumps. I enjoyed myself thoroughly, speculating on our average speed. The driver was a good sport, courteous and kind, though we could not speak to each other. He stopped short at a caravanserai, ushered me in, ordered lunch and, in real style, brought me a basin and slender-necked ewer and poured water over my hands. He was immensely amused, tried to teach me a few Persian words, and explained his version of the story to the other guests lunching in the garden. They soon collected around me while one, in halting French, tried to find out the reasons for this solitary journey.

At four o'clock I banged on my friends' door; they were amazed and delighted at the sight of the camera.

On this Feast of Spring the 'Sizdè', the skies remained stubbornly overcast and a chilly wind blew across the plain. Was it an echo of the political situation? Instead of dressing in their finery, people wore dark clothes, looking sullen and oppressed. Where were the gay crowds? the care-free picnickers? the beautiful white and coloured veils of bygone photographs? In this dull grey light, dark blue seemed, this year, the favourite colour.

Dense crowds surged on the banks of the river and collected on the bridges; entire families spread their carpets and settled on each loggia for the day. The nut and melon vendors plied their trade; pushing their hand-carts, they were, as usual, the centre of brisk business. Now and then, a solitary flute could be heard above the hum of the crowd and the rush of the waters. Policemen, discreet and easy-going, walked around.

At first, people were amused and mildly curious; kids peered into my camera; mothers pushed their babies towards the lenses. Slowly,

I made my way across the bridge, a handsome policeman acting amiably as escort. The crowd thickened; the atmosphere grew tense and the word 'Yankee', often repeated, was not meant as a compliment. I was jostled about, playfully at first, then, little by little, in excited mood. Fists were raised and pushed in my face, my camera was hit. But my handsome policeman did not forget his self-appointed job. He signalled to his comrades and soon I was surrounded and firmly walked back to the car.

PASARGADAE AND PERSEPOLIS

NOMADS have always ranged the hills of Persia and, already thousands of years ago in the plains and mountains of Fars, Cyrus the Great's forefathers had gathered under their rule most of the chieftains. We saw the nomads encamped where this monarch dwelt, and where his tomb still stands. Their black tents were pitched in every nook and cranny at the foot of the cliffs; flocks were traversing and climbing the steep rocks while others were already being milked.

On a slope, on the western side of this plain, the ruins of Pasargadae's fort are slowly re-emerging from the sands. Huge blocks of stone cover its walls, and the traditional design of the Achaemenian rose was brought to light while we were there.

In the middle of this fertile landscape, the remnants of a high monument – now fallen in ruins – appears like a tower and is perhaps Cambyses' tomb. If so, this tomb never served its purpose for Cambyses disappeared in Syria while returning from waging war against the Egyptians.

Further away, lies another mausoleum. From this distance, in the immensity of the Persian landscape, Cyrus' tomb is a squat, white unimportant building. It is hard to realise its really colossal proportions, and the only way to do so is to climb the massive steps that lead into the upper chamber. This, in itself, is quite difficult, for the margin of these stone slabs is narrow, and it is not easy to get a hold. The funeral chamber was, of course, plundered by thieves who were attracted and tempted by the fabulous wealth that, undoubtedly, was buried with the monarch. It is called the Masjid Mader-è-Suleiman (the mosque of the Mother of Solomon) and is still used as a diminutive mosque by those who are nimble enough to climb to this lofty sanctuary.

The tomb must have been an imposing monument, surrounded as it was by rows of columns. Like those of Persepolis, these have been broken by earthquakes, and pieces of them carried away by peasants whose custom it has been for generations to slice them up and put them to use as millstones. This has been done all over the East.

Nearby, the sites of three palaces were cleared in 1950-51. They offer little interest to the occasional tourist, though one or two sculptures are of great beauty, the most important being the 'Winged Genii'. The tail of a fish, of grey-blue stone, proves that here, as in Mesopotamia, the fish was the symbol of an honoured god.

Here and there in the flat plain, mounds of earth are to be seen. Called 'Tell' by archaeologists, many have already been excavated, yielding sometimes a precious crop of pottery, stone and other objects of an early age. For men come and go, the seasons alter, yet, inexorably, the sands of the desert shift and blow, and sooner or later cover up all landmarks.

We spent unforgettable hours in Pasargadae. Tired and exhausted we sought rest in a garden whose owner remained unknown, but to whom I shall always be grateful. In the hot and dusty plain it seemed just another mud-wall girdling a cluster of trees; but when we passed the gate, it was as if we had been allowed to enter a corner of paradise.

All was quiet and secluded . . . lovely rugs had been spread in the shade . . . water was boiling in the samovar . . . lunch was ready . . . tea was being served. Refreshed and at ease I lay on a carpet; overhead, the tall poplars bowed and swayed in the breeze, slender trunks white on the deep blue sky, leaves shimmering and rustling . . . Clouds floated lazily by.

As was our wont, we were late and arrived at Persepolis, – 'Takht-è-Jamshid', the 'Throne of Jamshid', legendary king, as the Persians call it – long after dark.

Yedda, taking me by the hand, guided me through the ruins. I could but guess at the broken columns, at the mass of fallen stones. Groping, we climbed the low and easy steps of the monumental stairway. As we emerged onto the immense terrace the clouds that were now blowing across the sky parted, and the moon shone down upon the landscape, breathtaking in the still solitary night. The huge columns towered above us, some of them damaged, twisted by earthquakes, standing precariously at amazing angles.

Next morning, and for many days to come, I was to get acquainted with the various halls and palaces that form the intricate complex of the Royal Town. All those who admire ancient art, and Achaemenian art in particular, have studied reproductions of the numerous and diverse reliefs sculptured on the famed royal stairway.

As, during this journey, I was especially interested in tribal life, it seemed to me significant that already, two thousand five hundred years ago, reverence and obedience to the sovereign ruler of the day should be expressed in this procession of familiar, domesticated animals. The beautiful horses, necks arched, reined in, prancing, led and tended by grooms; the majestic and disdainful camel, its nose pierced by its leading-rope, aloof and supercilious; a very elaborately horned goat; realistic rams; all walking towards the monarch's throne.

For long André, and other archaeologists before him, had been puzzled by a certain weird-looking animal. What could it be? Was it possible that these clever and talented sculptors had been obliged to sacrifice to the shape of the steps, distorting the figure they wanted to model? It seemed incredible. Yet, what ever was it? An elongated zebra? . . a foreshortened giraffe? Had these masters in realistic sculpture for once failed? And suddenly, months later in Paris, remembering a conversation with my son, it dawned upon me. I looked it up in a dictionary with Yedda, and I was right. This odd-looking, long-nosed, slouching animal, was none other than the now nearly extinct okapi. Some of us may recall that many years ago one of these species had been discovered in the Belgian Congo and offered, as a royal gift, to the Prince of Wales. Had this animal, twenty-five centuries ago, found its way through Africa, to walk, led by an Ethiopian, in the royal procession of Persepolis?

With André and Yedda we would examine, study and photograph, walking back and forth through the ruins and the sunbaked court-yards. The stairway – now protected by roofing, for its very fragile stone, hidden for centuries by mounds of earth, crumbles easily away – can only be well photographed in the very early hours. Six o'clock found us on the first steps: measurements taken, cameras set on their tripods—waiting. The sun, screened by the mountains, appeared and lit up the famous sculptures.

Quiet in the midday heat, huge green lizards scurried down

the stones as we approached, and the dried pods of wild-flowers rustled as they went into hiding.

At sunset, we would walk along the edge of the terrace and look down on the plain below. The big flagstones, in the evening light, took on a golden hue. Far away, in the distance, stood several massive rocks, one known as the Fortress of Istakhr.

Persepolis, the royal abode, destroyed by Alexander's vengeance, abandoned through the centuries, was little by little and day after day patiently being brought to light.

During the spring months, the spell of rainy weather gave to the plain an unusual aspect. Great clouds rolled over the horizon and hung low on the hills; storms broke; thunder boomed and reverberated on the barren rocks; the desert lost its desolate appearance: covered with tufts of grass it changed into one immense green field through which the flocks of the nomad tribes roamed constantly. The shepherds drove them on relentlessly, for the rains interfering with their normal routine had forced them to seek shelter day after day. From usually dried springs water, this year, ran freely, and the smallest ditch or brook became a flowing stream.

In Persepolis, on the terrace of the Apadana, flowers peeped up from between the stones; large pools formed, and the stately columns were reflected in these unexpected mirrors. In spite of rain and mud, excavation work continued.

Below the terrace, at a distance of about half a mile, close to a big building which is still almost entirely buried and is probably the palace in which Darius actually lived, another Royal building was found a year ago. It was thrilling to walk there with André, to have him explain Achaemenian architecture and to see the inscription on the base of one of the columns: 'Xerxes the King has said: I built this Tatchara.'

It was exciting too to stand near a newly dug pit and to watch, slowly emerging from its bed of clay, first the head of an eagle, then, a yard and a half away, another one identical to the first, then the stone block serving as body to the two heads, then finally a paw.* This was a curious discovery: for the first time in Achaemenian architecture, a griffon of this kind was the decorative motive of a capital of a column. We slid down into the pit and decided that by our

* See article in *Illustrated London News*, January 2nd, 1954.

standards it was not a success. André was, however, interested by what he considered 'an authentic example of a typical mistake'. He pointed out that, from below, one would only have seen the bulky geometrical body ending on either side with a pointed form, the enormous beaks of the two-headed bird; this would have seemed incomprehensible and meaningless, and André considered that those who were building the 'Takht' took the same view. This model of a new capital had probably been rejected, and abandoned in the sculptors' work-shop where we now stood.

In comparison with the splendid bulls' heads that became one of the chief adornments of Achaemenian palaces, this griffon seemed indeed a poor caricature!

Was Persepolis ever beautiful? Personally, I doubt it. Majestic, impressive, fear-inspiring to those who were admitted in the sove-reign's presence – certainly: but not beautiful. The visitor arriving at sun-down in Baalbek is awed by the ethereal ruins. But in its day it too must have been an oppressive mass of sculptured stone. Persepolis struck me as being in similar bad taste. André patiently explained the architectural feat; and as they now stand, the fragments of the broken columns are a wonderful sight. But when one considers the fact that each of these was topped by a capital of grimacing or solemn heads; that these were not of the mellow golden colour that the centuries have given them, but some, like those in the Teheran Museum, were highly polished, dark grey or nearly black, others probably painted in garish and varied tones, the result must have been frightening.

In the glare of the midday sun, the Egyptian Pyramids seem drably overwhelming; the desert is flat, dull and monotonous. The terrace of Persepolis seen from a distance, loses its majesty and appears a jumble of fragmented and stranded pillars. Perspective is lost; the empty and derelict courtyards dismal in their array of broken stones. For Persepolis, tragically burnt by Alexander the Great in a moment of destructive fury and vengeance, suffered later from numerous earthquakes.

When the first rays of the morning sun shine from over the hill, they touch first one, then another sculpture. Suddenly as if by magic, Persepolis awakens. Darius, in his majesty, seated on his throne, holds in his hands the symbols of power and of eternal life:

the royal sceptre and the lotus of wisdom and of immortality. His courtiers and warriors, facing him, mount their everlasting guard, and the procession of gift-bearers and of familiar animals with the oft repeated and celebrated motive of the lion attacking a bull marches forward.

In the evening, in the glory of the slanting rays, we would climb the hill and look upon the ruined city. High above, hewn out of the rocks, are the tombs of the last Achaemenians. From these lofty places, in the clear air, each detail was visible: the neat rows of the column bases stood out like checker-boards, their shadows lengthening and deepening in the failing light.

We would sit on the barren stones, or in a tiny garden, perched on the hillside, known to us as 'Mary Helen's garden' and touchingly tended as a tribute to the memory of the wife of Eric Schmidt – Head of the Chicago Mission from 1934 to 1939 – who, living there for years and devoting her time to art and science, had with her own hands created it in this rocky desert.

Sometimes we would forsake the Royal Palaces and go for long treks in the plain; past the city of Istakhr, where only a few blocks of stone mark the site of a once flourishing town. Beyond the river, on the face of the 'Husain Kuh', at 'Naksh-è-Rustem', huge crosses have been cut in the rock. Carved in their centres are the openings to the funeral chambers of some royal tombs, among them those of Darius and Xerxes. The tops of these forbidding monuments are decorated with the familiar frieze depicting the king, upheld by the peoples of the Empire, praying in front of a fire-altar, under the aegis of the god Ahura-Mazda. The details of some of the figures of tribesmen are stylised in a remarkable way. The figure of the monarch is conventional, and the image of the god amusing and naïve – he seems to be carried through the air in a very primitive flying machine consisting of a pair of wings.

This cliff is marked by many other historical relics: reliefs of Elamite, Sasanian, Parthian times have been engraved side by side; a Mazdean fire-altar is but a few yards away; at the bend of the track, in a small grotto, is an 'Imamzadè' still honoured by Muslim pilgrims. Further still, at the end of the valley, the horizon is barred by the strangely shaped hill called the Fortress of Istakhr. In the sixteenth century, Shah Ismail was imprisoned in the citadel built

The horse lines at the camp of Khosrow-Shirin

Kashkai, wearing their typical hats, on the threshold of their tents

on its summit. Did this beautiful landscape fill his soul with patience and serenity? We called it the 'Happy Valley', for peaceful and blessed were our moments there.

One day, exploring the rocks beyond the royal tombs, we found some nomads encamped in deep grottos. We had been lured to this site, known as Hajji-Abad, by a wish to see an ancient Pahlevi inscription that is carved on the inner wall. This text, deciphered by Sylvestre de Sacy at the end of the eighteenth century, was essential in the reading of all other Pahlevi texts.

Far above the valley, at the entrance of the grotto, children were playing in the dust. Under the rocky vault, in semi darkness, women in scarlet robes were milking gigantic black goats that seemed to us, in these strange surroundings, the incarnation of Beelzebub.

At other times we would roam the countryside. The nomads were everywhere on the march during the early hours of the day. We found them, one morning, crossing the dam of Band-è-Amir. This remarkable construction holds back the waters of the Kur river, and is said to be very ancient.

We also often met nomads on the main road, where the careful shepherds drove their cattle along, preventing them from straying into the vast fields of sugar-beet. As soon as they had passed the fertile plains, they would spread out fan-wise into the desert, grazing as they went. The flocks were always carefully separated and kept in small groups. They were gregarious and showed little tendency to straggle. When frightened by an approaching car or truck they would however, start off, scurrying up a slope or scattering in the valley, spreading like a tidal wave over moors and rocks.

The sheep-dogs are of a typical breed. Their coat is long; sometimes light in colour, often pure white or creamy, flecked with dun, sometimes quite black. They are large, though smaller than a Saint Bernard, but of similar build, swift and sturdy. Their sole duty, I am told, is to ward off the wolves that are plentiful in the mountains. Unlike collies or other sheep-dogs, they do not circle their charges constantly, but trot along with the flock. They are part of it, accepted by the shepherds who do not ill-treat them. Yet I have never seen them caressed or fondled, though the pups, when still too weak and small to walk, are carried around together with the tribes' babies and the new-born lambs. They would be handsome, except for one thing: their ears are trimmed, cut clean off near the skull. This is not done out of cruelty. On the contrary it is a precaution against wolves who might otherwise tear them to pieces during a fight.

Dogs seem as a rule to be treated with indifference. Some fabulously thin ones hung around the Persepolis ruins and were fed scraps of food by a kind-hearted and talented Russian artist who was working on an amazingly accurate model of the palaces. It was fascinating to see him copy, on a very small scale, the gigantic sculptures and reliefs. Each day the dogs, scared of the servants, would sneak to his door, shivering with expectation and impatience. A pathetically thin bitch crawled up among the others. We shared the same terrace and, one morning, I saw that she had been followed by an even thinner pup. One eye on the servants' door, for I feared their anger, I poured a few drops of milk into a crack in the pavement. Ravenously, the mother lapped it up while the pup looked hungrily on, too frightened to move. They returned the next day, and when I fed them, the miserable mother snarled, and, snapping, chased her pup away.

This was too much. When she had eaten her fill, I chased her in my turn, hoping that the poor, unfortunate pup might risk coming back. It did, and though it took me several days of patient coaxing, it eventually entered my room as I threw pieces of bread closer and closer to the table. One morning I stretched out and patted it gently. And suddenly it discovered the joy of being loved, the kindness of the human hand and touch. In ecstacy it flung itself upon me, licking my face and neck, then rolled onto its back to be caressed again; then, leaping into the air, it ran around in circles till it threw itself once more upon me.

Never have I seen such boundless joy, and never have I forgiven myself: for, thoughtlessly, I had given what I could never give again, revealing happiness and then withdrawing it. As we drove away, unable to carry the poor beast on a long and tedious journey, I could not bear to look back.

We had heard of these dogs' bad reputation: travellers, as a rule, feared their attacks, and even intrepid Freya Stark fell victim to their fierceness: 'To keep the dogs off their visitors is one of the chief preoccupations of the tribal host. I was always absent-minded, and not inclined to be afraid of dogs, and gave constant uneasiness. . . I set off to turn back without remembering the dogs, who, seeing a swiftly moving object, flung themselves on me in a body, and had my skirt in shreds in no time. The tribe hurled clods of earth and curses, while I stood still among their unpleasant fangs, and the men drew near, beating their breasts, with horrified faces. "That this should have happened in our tents" they repeated again and again. The dogs turned snarling away... "Why do you run" said the Philosopher (her guide), "and get bitten by dogs, so that I am made anxious?"'

Was it because, heavily laden, I could not run fast, or did my tripod seem to the dogs a formidable weapon? Though in Persepolis, and later among the tribes, I walked right in the midst of flocks and herds, I was never molested.

In the evenings, camps being pitched all over the plain, we would wander around the nomads' tents. To them we must appear equally strange, and we astonished them by our curiosity. They clustered about us, laughing and joking among themselves, showing us the young lambs born that very day, that were, they hoped, to fetch a good price on the wool and fur market in Shiraz. The district is famous for its 'Astrakhan', better known nowadays as 'Persian Lamb'.

I had brought with me some special torches, hoping to use them for filming at night. With some misgivings, I broached the subject, wondering if I dare turn a patch of the dark desert into a dazzling inferno? The nomads, mildly curious, did not seem to mind; but what might be the reactions of camels, goats and sheep? Would the children scream with fright? We set the camera, and lit the torches. Held at arms length, they burnt fiercely, throwing a brilliant light. Amazed at first, the children looked on in silent wonder. Then, mouths agape, started clapping their hands in glee. Women, their babies in their arms, drew close, enjoying this unknown sight. This was to be their first and only display of fireworks.

When, next morning, we met once more on the road, we had become friends, and were greeted by cheers and smiles.

Part II

ON THE KASHKAI TRAIL

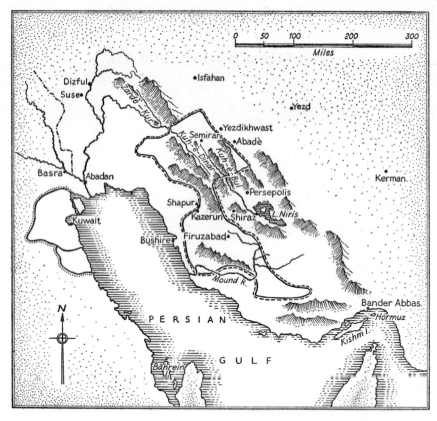

Southern Persia and the area over which the Kashkai migrate.

NOMAD

If dust dries thy brow
Or the desert sun burns thine eyes,
Remember that soft will be the evening light
And cool the waters of the spring.

If thy friend has left thee
And if loneliness is hard to bear,
Remember that at dawn the lark will sing
And the nightingale call plaintively
During the dark hours of the night.

If the stones on the trail wound thy feet
Remember that the world over one must suffer and endure.

And if the road of life seems long and painful
Remember that only once must it be travelled!

(While listening to a poem by Hafiz)

SHIRAZ AND FIRUZABAD

'TO Madame Jean Ullens – Hotel Park Sa'adi – Shiraz or Takht-è-Djamshid.

'All my thanks for your telegram. I shall be in Firuzabad till Friday. Unfortunately I·shall have to go into tribal territory after Friday. I shall be very glad if yourself, Monsieur and Madame André Godard will be my guests in Firuzabad for as many days as you wish. My agent in Firuzabad will be at your service.

'NASSER KASHKAI'

For several days we had been hoping and expecting this wire. In Persepolis, every morning at breakfast, or in the evening, we would ask each other: 'No news of Nasser Khan?' – 'No news'. . . Suddenly, one morning, Monsieur Sami, the Curator of Persepolis, told us that we were expected in Firuzabad. At last the telegram was delivered, and, soon after we were once more on our way, altering our plans and spending one night only in Shiraz.

We had been made to understand that we should be in Firuzabad for lunch. The road is long, and though we had left early, I insisted on losing precious minutes, and begged permission to spend a few moments in the Hafiziyè, the lovely garden where under an alabaster tombstone, the poet Hafiz lies. In spite of the very early hour, entire families were gathered there in pilgrimage; young students were pacing back and forth in the paths, meditating on their texts or on the perfection of a poem.

From the steps of the Hafiziyè terrace we looked at the town of Shiraz. The bulb-shaped domes of the mosques glistened in the morning sun, though a slight haze hung over the plain. Close by, a group of pines, clustered in a walled-in garden, cast their shadow on the Haft-Tan Monastery. We tried to overlook and to forget the hideous, huge and shiny petrol tanks that mar the entrance to this city whose name should remain the symbol of poetry and of gardens.

Tourists often complain about the Iranian roads, the bumpy surface, the dust. Few roads, it is true, are macadamised, but the experi-

PLATE 7 'Standing in the shadow of some majestic cupola,
we looked down upon the town'
Isfahan, from the roof of the Masjid-è-Shah, the Royal Mosque (Page 32)

PLATE 8   André Godard climbing the Tomb of Cyrus the Great
(Page 35)

PLATE 9   'The huge columns towered above us.'   Persepolis (Page 36)

PLATE 10   'The splendid bull's head, adornment of this
            Achaemenian palace' (Page 39)

'For the first time in Achaemenian architecture, a griffon of this
kind was the decorative motive (Page 38)

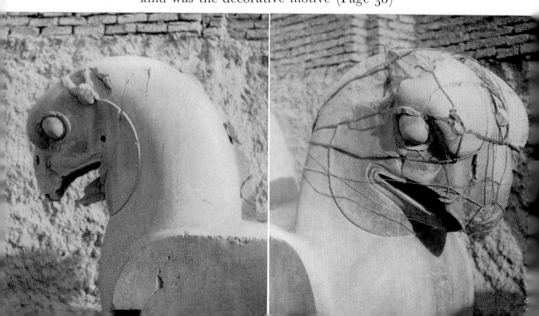

enced driver is able to maintain an excellent average speed, and the main highways, at least, are kept in constant repair. I admired the teams of workmen who often far from their villages, in line by the road-side, would all day long rake, with their long-handled tools, levelling dust and gravel in spite of the sun and the sometimes hard-blowing winds.

But that morning, the torrential rains of the past days had rendered the Firuzabad highway unfit for travel. I was reminded of an appropriate sentence, quoted by Professor Mallowan: 'What is a road?' – 'It is a track men carefully avoid in rainy weather'. . . . We slipped and skidded, and the passing cars and buses sprayed us with mud. Every few miles the driver stopped, stepped gingerly from the car and tried to find a pool of clean water, then carefully washed the windscreen. During the first two hours, we averaged fifteen miles per hour; later, though the road improved, when we started taking photos, this fell to twelve or ten. Would we ever reach Firuzabad?

After a while the road, leaving the Shiraz valley, climbed into the hills. The water was drained by the slope and we managed to gather speed; but we were penetrating into tribal territory, and huge flocks on the march barred our way. Ahead of us were steep mountains; at the entrance of a rocky defile the waters of a spring called 'Ab-è-Bahram' were running swiftly and shimmering on red boulders.

The road wound through high cliffs. Spread out in scenery that reminded one of Persian miniatures were black goats'-hair tents. Once more I begged permission to linger. I wanted to film. But I knew that André, who is precision incarnate, might soon become impatient. So we started off again, to land straight into the migrating crowd: flock after flock passed on this narrow road that overhangs deep gulleys. As each new group came marching on we were forced to halt and let the flow of camels, goats, and sheep go by: we did not want to cause stampede or panic. Delighted by these forced stops, I filmed continuously, climbed back into the car, jumped out again after having driven on a few yards only. Yedda's camera was as busy as mine.

We were completely surrounded by a mass of grumbling, bleating animals, scared by the noise of the engines. We were not alone on

D

the road: ahead of us a huge oil-tanker blocked the way and we were closely followed by a lorry. Some camels broke loose, left the track and jumped clumsily down from rock to rock, heedless of the risk they were running. They looked grotesque as they waddled down the slope and I did my best to photograph them, but was, alas, not quick enough. The nomads seemed to take all this as a matter of course. They were joyful and smiling as they went by, shouting to encourage their beasts.

The car's clock hands turned relentlessly. At what time would we eventually arrive? Slowly, stopping repeatedly, we covered these few miles, meandering through rocky mountains, narrow defiles, then down an impressively steep slope amid wooded hills. These green forests, in total contrast with the usually barren soil of the Iranian landscape, struck our fancy, as did the joyful, smiling tribesmen.

Suddenly, miraculously, the crowd dispersed, vanished, and the road was deserted. Where were these multitudes of herds, and where were their escorts? A solitary traveller remained by the road-side, his pipe carefully tucked away in his collar. Later, I found out that migration always takes place in the early morning, the march lasting only a few hours, and covering from ten to twenty-five miles. This, of course, depends on the configuration of the land and the condition of the pastures. The rest of the day is usually spent in pitching camp, and tending the flocks. The ewes are milked, butter is churned in goats skins, curds, rolled into small balls, are set in the sun to dry. They will come in handy for the winter supply. The women devote themselves to home work, spinning wool, or weaving tribal rugs on looms that are quickly set up.

The road entered a new gorge, narrower and more abrupt than the first, yet perhaps more beautiful still. Down below the torrent flowed, its waters blue and clear. To-morrow, we decided, we must manage to come back to this point at a moment when the road would be cluttered by the migrating tribes.

We were only slightly late; we stopped short at the gates of the Kashkai Chief's home; driving under the archway, we found ourselves in a garden where huge poppies were in full bloom. Greeted by several people, we were told that Nasser Khan was visiting one of his brothers, in the neighbourhood. He would be coming shortly. Without even being given the opportunity to wash our hands and freshen up a bit, we were ushered into a lounge with modern European furniture; walls adorned by paintings of the 1880 era: Cairo, seen from the Citadel, and the portrait of an ancestor. Tea was carried in, then, soon after, we were invited to cross the terrace onto which opens the dining-room, bare-walled and sparsely furnished: a long table, chairs, a sideboard, and a large and up-to-date frigidaire that must be most useful in this climate. Seats were set for a number of guests, and large dishes of 'pilaw' were already served. We never ate a really hot meal during our stay.

People came and went, the door swung to and fro, dishes were brought in or carried out . . . Once more the door opened; André and Yedda rose to their feet: it was Nasser Khan Kashkai. Very tall, erect, powerfully built; high forehead, aquiline nose; truly an impressive figure. When later, I knew him better, I learnt to appreciate his judgement, his moderation, his thoughtfulness. Apologising for not having been there to greet us, he joined us at our meal, but ate quickly and sparingly as, I soon found out, is his habit.

Malek Mansur Kashkai, his brother, turned up a few minutes later. A former student of Oxford and Reading Colleges, he speaks perfect English. Because he is wiry and much thinner than his brother, he seems even taller. Years spent hunting in the mountains have etched fine wrinkles around his eyes. His sharp features and high cheekbones are stressed by dark eyebrows and humorous, sensitive lips. When questioned, and before answering, he has an amusing trick of quickly passing his open hand over his face, from forehead to chin, as if drawing a veil over his countenance.

We all finished lunch together, then Nasser Khan invited us to walk around the garden and watch the tribeswomen busily weaving rugs. Their loom is set up under a large tent, and is made of long wooden poles, placed near the ground. Nasser Khan had the tent-flaps lifted so that we should have sufficient light for pictures and photographs. In the centre of the tent, kneeling in a single line, the women bent over their work; their hands moved back and forth. Their dresses were beautiful: tight-fitting bodices, ample and many coloured skirts. On the tent ropes hung gay bunches of vivid hued skeins of wool.

Not far from there, and near the garden gate, a group of men stood waiting. Nasser Khan walked towards them. This was a good occasion for filming different groups: an aged hunter had just brought, in homage to his Chief, a wild sheep shot in the nearby hills. It was a fine trophy: its horns were magnificently curved. I was told that this hunter, who still wore the ancient coat and rounded skull cap, had been a very famous warrior. Close by, a big bundle of grass was carefully carried, then set on the ground: from it emerged two wobbly, minute, pathetically weak and young wild boars. They had just been caught in their lair! They would not be killed, but reared in the Khan's stables, as playmates for his horses. This is a very old custom, originating in the belief that boars are able to avert the 'evil eye'.

The afternoon was spent peacefully in the garden, chatting and sipping countless glasses of tea. The Firuzabad climate, though very warm in summer, is particularly mild in winter and spring: beneath the swaying fronds of palms, cherry-trees, rose bushes and poppies were in bloom. Flies and bees buzzed lazily from flower to flower, their drone a perfect music for all this loveliness. Through the arch-way, the bare hills were blue in the shimmering light.

We lived according to Iranian custom: supper was served late at night. But before this, we were shown to our rooms: André was to sleep on a camp-bed in the lounge; Yedda and I shared the guest-room near-by; it was bare of furniture save for two vast, old-fashioned bedsteads, supporting two very small mattresses. This was going to cause us trouble. Both of us absent-minded and rather untidy, we left our clothes lying, at random, on the beds. They would slip off and disappear under the mattresses, where some of them still are perhaps. . .

To ensure our privacy while dressing in the evening, we had to turn off the light, for our bedroom windows had neither shutters nor blinds, and servants kept walking up and down the terrace. Later, when in the Kashkai camp, I remembered the habit, acquired in India, of becoming indifferent to these ubiquitous presences.

Though we seemed to have chatted endlessly with our hosts, I knew that the evening hours would be spent in conversation. I was determined to make the most of them and to get all possible information about the Kashkai Tribes. This is what Malek Mansur told me:

'To survive, nomads have been always obliged to fight. They

lead a wandering life and do not accumulate documents and archives.

'But in the evenings, around fires that are burning low, the elders will relate striking events, deeds of valour in which the tribes pride themselves. Thus the epic tale is told from father to son, down through the ages.

'The tribes of Central Asia were forced by wars, strife, upheavals, to abandon their steppes and seek new pasture grounds . . . so the Huns, the Visigoths, and before them the Aryans, had invaded India, Iran, Europe.

'When Jengis Khan set forth as "Conqueror of the World" the eddies of his wars and battles sent new waves of unrest across the Asian plateau.

'The Turks, forsaking the regions where they had dwelt for centuries, started moving down through the Turan and Caspian depressions, establishing themselves eventually on the frontiers of the Iranian Empire and in Asia Minor.

'We are of Turkish language and race; some say that we are descendants of the Turkish Ghuzz Tribe, known for its cruelty and fierceness, and that our name is derived from the Turkish "Kashka" meaning "a horse with a white star on its forehead". Others think this name indicates that we came from Kashgar in the wake of Hulagu. Others still that it means "fugitive".

'Though these versions differ, we believe that the arrival of our Tribes in Iran coincided with the conquests of Jengis Khan, in the thirteenth century. Soon after, our ancestors established themselves on the slopes of the Caucasus. We are descendants of the "Tribe of the Ak Koyunlu" the "Tribe of the White Sheep" famed for being the only tribe in history capable of inflicting a defeat on Tamerlane. For centuries we dwelt on the lands surrounding Ardebil, but, in the first half of the sixteenth century we settled in southern Persia, Shah Ismail having asked our warriors to defend this part of the country against the intrusions of the Portuguese. Thus, our Tribes came to the Province of Fars, near the Persian Gulf, and are still only separated from it by a ridge of mountains, the Makran.

'The yearly migrations of the Kashkai, seeking fresh pastures, drive them from the south to the north, where they move to their summer quarters "Yeilak" in the high mountains; and from the north to the south, to their winter quarters, "Qishlaq".

'In summer, the Kashkai flocks graze on the slopes of the Kuh-è-Dinar; a group of mountains from 12,000 to 15,000 feet, that are a part of the Zagros chain.

'In autumn the Kashkai break camp, and by stages leave the highlands. They winter in the warmer regions near Firuzabad, Kazerun, Jerrè, Farashband, on the banks of the river Mound, till, in April, they start once more on their yearly trek.

'The migration is organised and controlled by the Kashkai Chief. The Tribes carefully avoid villages and towns such as Shiraz and Isfahan, lest their flocks, estimated at seven million head, might cause serious damage. This annual migration is the largest of any Persian tribe.

'It is difficult to give exact statistics, but we believe that the Tribes now number 400,000 men, women and children.'

The conversation then switched on to big-game hunting, and suddenly I aroused Malek Mansur's interest. I told him of our adventures in the Rocky Mountains and the Scandinavian highlands; of my experience of horses and horsemanship. Gradually the conversation altered, lost its conventional form, and became the intimate, easy-going chatter of old friends. I felt that my hopes might be fulfilled and that perhaps the goal I had secretly aimed at was in sight. Listening to us, Nasser Khan turned to me and said:

'I have never allowed anyone to film my Tribes. I was offered sums of money. I have refused. You, a woman, have travelled thousands of miles in this hope. Do as you please, here in Firuzabad. But it is late in the season; the migration, in this part of the country, is over. If, in about three weeks, the political situation permitting, you wish to visit us in our spring camp of Khosrow-Shirin, do so. You will see our pastures, our springs, and our snow-covered mountains . . . you will see our horses . . . and you can live with us, in our tents.'

I thanked him with a smile. Nothing could have pleased me more! In the bottom of my heart I vowed not to rest till I had managed to get to Khosrow-Shirin.

We dined together and were served the same food: rice and 'kebab.' Soon after, we decided to go to bed; immediately we were plunged in darkness, as each evening the dynamo of the electric plant was stopped.

At about six o'clock next morning, I wandered off into the garden where I wanted to film the flowers and the scenery in peace and quiet.

The night before we had met Khosrow Khan, the younger brother, then deputy in Teheran, and had asked after his mother. He had told us that she was ailing. At this very early hour, and to my absolute astonishment, she stepped out of a car. Supported by her youngest son and extremely frail, nevertheless she stood erect with the natural inborn dignity and grace of a very great lady. Her eyes are pensive and her mouth is sad. Yet her face is extremely beautiful, though etched by years of hardship and a life spent in the wind and sun of the high mountains. She was dressed in grey, the colour of mourning, having known the sorrows of life and of tragic widowhood. A flowing cape over a simple dress, and a silk veil, were her only attire.

Immediately interested in my work, she told her sons that they must show me their camps. They might, perhaps, after all, have hesitated to repeat their invitation. Later, when all seemed difficult, I saw her again; encouraged by her, I risked the journey. I wonder if, otherwise, I would have undertaken it.

In spite of the very early hour, the atmosphere in the garden seemed uneasy. Was the political situation deteriorating? Conversations were going on in agitated whispers. Nobody objected when we begged leave to get on our way, and a guide was amiably provided.

Off once more, on the road to Tang-è-Ab. The herds and flocks were on the move; we had to by-pass and get ahead if we were to film them on the march. We had to be careful; we did not want to frighten the animals or hinder the shepherds. Time and time again, we saw them during the morning hours. They arrived in throngs, pushed on by the impatient crowd, jammed up against each other in this narrow defile. Astride their horses, women, armed with rifles and carbines, their skirts spread out over the horses' backs, held themselves proudly. They often carried in their arms a baby or a small child still too weak to walk who, in his turn, held on to a lamb or a kid born that same morning. Often too, another child, riding pillion, clung to his mother's waist. These women sometimes even managed to keep on spinning as they rode. Now and again an armed rider, smart and handsome, escorted them.

Girls and youths, laughing and shouting, drove the herds along. We avoided them carefully, for they might have bolted and fallen headlong down the rocky slope. Too small still to keep up with the others, closing the march, groups of young and weak lambs and kids trotted along on their wobbly legs, led by tiny tots whose size was pathetic in the vast landscape.

Finally, bearing old men and women whose faces were deeply furrowed by innumerable wrinkles, came the procession of humble donkeys. Piled upon their patient backs were huge cauldrons for boiling rice, domestic odds and ends, puppies crouching on their feeble paws, cocks and hens precariously perched, wildly flapping their wings to retain their balance; while disdainful and aloof, the camels, bearing tents and colourful carpets, marched on in single file.

So, faithful to tradition and custom, its hope in the fertility of the soil and the bounty of heaven, courageous and gay, yet submitting to its fate, this horde has moved across mountains and valleys for thousands of years.

For a picture-hunter this was really paradise; light was perfect; the scenery worthy of the most famous miniature painters; the colours enchanting. I ran around frantically, took a bad fall as, trying to catch up with a group hidden by cliffs, down near the river, I got the tripod of my camera jammed between stones. In spite of a severely gashed leg, I picked myself up quickly, ran, helped along by the guide, and joined the crowd as it was crossing; climbed onto my rocky perch again. The minutes flew. By noon, the last groups had spread out in the plain. Yet, I was not satisfied. Would they come by on the morrow?

We set out, once more, soon after lunch, and retraced our steps on the now familiar road. The long avenue, edged by huge rose bushes – the glories of the south – leads straight towards the fort, built high on top of a knoll. The site of Firuzabad seems a succession of gardens, protected by mud-walls, above which the fronds of palm and date trees tower and sway. The garden of Bibi Khanum, Nasser Khan's mother, was pointed out to us from far off; the rows of cypress trees, nearly two hundred years old, planted by one of their ancestors, stood out against the sky.

PLATE 11   'The spell of rainy weather gave to the plain an unusual aspect'
The ruins of Persepolis (Page 38)

Photo: *André Godard*

PLATE 12 One of Darius' warriors. Persepolis (the Royal Stairway)
(Page 40)

PLATE 13   'A lion attacking a bull'
Detail from the Royal Stairway at Persepolis (Page 40)

PLATE 14 'We called it "the Happy Valley"' (Page 41)

Close to the city itself, modern, spotlessly white buildings: new school, and hospital, built by the initiative of Nasser Khan and of Bibi Khanum.

At the foot of the grey-blue hills, in the distance, a mound rising above the plain: ruins of a fire-altar built by Ardeshir near the town called, in his time, Jur or Gur. In the tenth century, Abu-Ishak-al-Istakhri wrote: 'Jur was built by Ardeshir on ground that was covered by stagnant water. This king had vowed to build a city and a "Pyrée" on the spot where he was waging war and where he would be victorious. It was precisely at Gūr that he won this victory. He drained the soil, then built the town he called Jur. This town is nearly as big as Istakhr, Shapur and Darabgird; it is surrounded by a well preserved earthen wall and a moat. It has four gates. In the centre of the town is a building in the shape of a platform, called Tirbal by the Arabs, and known by the Persians as Iwan and Kiya Khurrè. It was built by Ardeshir and it is said that it rose so high that from its summit one could see the entire city and the surrounding country. The king also had an aqueduct made to bring water from the opposite mountain to the fire-alter on the summit of the platform. The Tirbal is an edifice made of stone and mortar. The greater part has been taken by the inhabitants for their own use; a small part alone has survived.'

The banks of the Barazè river, at the entrance of the Firuzabad defile, are dotted with historical ruins. On the northern side, the palace of Ardeshir, the Sasanian king, stands in majestic solitude; though never restored throughout 2,000 years, it remains as the centuries pass. Its derelict courtyards stable the roaming horses or goats of the nomads, and the powerful arches still uphold the crumbling brickwork.

In the morning we had met Nasser Khan's beautiful thoroughbreds as they were being led to the mountain camps. None now could be provided for us. So we had to leave the car, and ford the river on foot. This, in itself, was no feat, for though we were in spring and the season rainy, the water was low. In a warm climate it is always a delight to see it flow over rounded pebbles, clear and shimmering in the sunlight, and to feel its coolness on one's feet and ankles. But, carrying my heavy tripod and cameras, I was often afraid of slipping.

These fast-flowing rivers always reminded me of the Persian princess who, having married the Great Moghul, and in spite of all the riches he laid at her feet, longed for the turbulent and fresh torrents of her native mountains. Because the emperor loved her dearly, the still waters of the palace pools were made to flow over marble steps cut into special patterns, simulating, as they fell into the tanks below, the graceful movement of the leaping trout. Thus were imagined the lovely Shalimar Gardens, I was told.

The hours slid quietly by. The sun beat hot on the stones; light and shadow played on the rocks, enhancing the faces of long vanished sovereigns, carved high on the cliffs. These reliefs, a feature of Sasanian art, relate to the passing generations tales of power and of glory. The water was pellucid, and flowed deep-blue on the polished pebbles. Above the defile, buzzards circled ceaselessly, and the ruins of another Sasanian fort, jutted out on the topmost rocks, stood guard on the now quiet countryside. Save for the tinkling of running water, the call of a solitary bird, and the sound of crickets in the thorny bushes, all was silent in the afternoon heat.

As we turned again toward the Kashkai gardens, the skies were overcast, and the rays of the setting sun, slanting through dense clouds, outlined the distant mountains and the dark proud mass of the Firuzabad fort.

Nasser Khan's wire mentioned that he would be leaving Firuzabad on the day of our arrival. Had he changed his plans because of us, or was he delayed by political problems? That evening, we realised that he was greatly preoccupied: the hour was solemn. In Teheran, the Prime Minister was due to make a speech, and the radio was on all the time. The fate of Nasser Khan was at stake; his father had died in prison during Riza Shah Pahlevi's reign, and he himself had spent six years of his youth in captivity and exile. Tonight he spoke to us freely; he told us that the Tribes were becoming nervous. He wanted to join them, to keep them quiet and prevent them from doing anything rash.

So as to allow our hosts complete liberty, we discussed our plans among ourselves and decided to leave Firuzabad definitely at dawn, next day.

Once more, I woke up early and sneaked off to the garden. There is nothing I love better than the first solitary moments of dawn, when the world is young and at peace. There were many things I wanted to film. But I was not alone. Voices came from a clump of bushes: Nasser Khan, already surrounded by followers, was drinking tea with them.

With great courtesy, our hosts saw us off. As we took our leave, rolls of rugs were carried into the courtyard: presents from Nasser Khan and his mother, they were bundled into the car by the servants. We had not even time to admire them, but we managed to express our thanks before bowing ourselves off.

The political stress was such that, in spite of their natural hospitality and kindness, we sensed that our hosts were relieved. Already yesterday, while we were admiring their horses, they had told us that these were being sent in advance, far along the road, where they would catch them up by jeep. (The jeep, ugly but convenient, is now a familiar machine in Persia. It will bring comfort, and will ease the long and tedious journeys, but it will eventually kill the picturesque and poetic beauty of the migration.)

As we drove past, André cast a loving look on the beautiful, stately Sasanian ruin; Yedda and I gazed with regret at the abrupt ravine, the steep cliffs, the sculptured rocks, the blue and shallow river, in short all this Tang-è-Ab where we had spent such thrilling hours. Though it was still early, the place was deserted, and hoping that luck would come my way, I insisted on lingering awhile.

Leaving my friends on the bank, shouldering my tripod, I waded to the other shore, stumbling on the slippery stones. The djinns of desert and hills favoured me. . . Out of consideration for my patient friends I was ready to give up my vigil, for there was no soul or living animal in sight, when, from far above, clear and limpid in the silence, the sound of a mountain refrain, monotonous and nostalgic, was wafted on the waters. Soon after, making for the ford, their bells tinkling as they trotted along, came the flocks. They stopped for a long refreshing drink before crossing the river and gave me the opportunity of taking some very good shots.

On our way back to Shiraz the light was exquisite, and we spent the rest of the day covering this very short stage, dallying by the road side.

On that same evening I went to call on Khosrow Khan. We had often wandered in the Kashkai gardens of 'Bagh-è-Aram', the 'Garden of Heaven', admiring the stately trunks of the centenarian pines and the oldest, straightest and most beautiful cypresses of Iran. It amused me, that evening, to arrive there no longer as a tourist but as a guest!

Recognising me, the steward welcomed me with a smile and bade me enter. Though, during my previous visits, I had been interested and intrigued by the architecture and typical decorations of the Kashkai home, I had not been inside the house. It is, in fact, a small palace and was built during the reign of Fath-Ali Shah by one of Nasser Khan's ancestors. The building was finished by his grandfather. Three arches, ornamented by glazed tiles, the slender columns of the terrace, give it a truly Persian style. I did not go over the various reception rooms, but what I saw of the interior was in total contrast: the walls of halls and passages, painted in white, could have been those of the most modern nursing-home. I was introduced into a bare room, lit by stained-glass windows and furnished with comfortable sofas.

Khosrow Khan was in the garden, surrounded by friends. He looked preoccupied as he came to join me. He had arrived from Firuzabad a few hours earlier and had been receiving a steady stream of visitors; as deputy in the Teheran Chamber he was evidently deep in political discussion.

In spite of this, he momentarily put aside his cares and – probably in compliance with his mother's wishes – insisted I should go and visit the Tribes in the Beiza district where the tribal gathering was reputed to be particularly picturesque.

Calling to one of his followers whose name was Mohammed, and who spoke perfect English, he told him to look after me. 'But', he added, 'go first with your friends to Persepolis, and come back in four days' time, next Thursday. On Friday morning you will leave early with Mohammed. We are going to be very busy these coming days; many things may happen, and we must keep in contact with our more distant Tribes.'

Were we under a spell? Was it the magic of mountain scenery, pure air and clear streams, the real beauty of the Firuzabad region? In Shiraz, the atmosphere seemed to us oppressive, stifling, disagreeable. People were nervous, preoccupied; little incidents informed us of the political tension. This anxiousness, the timorous attitude of a few, became unbearable. Giving up the study of various historical monuments, casting but a glance on the charming buildings of the seventeenth century and of the Zend period, whose tiles of delicate pink, yellow, and light blue shades differ from the other Iranian 'kashi', yet rival them in beauty by the tracery of their intricate floral designs, we left the city.

The light that evening on the plain of Persepolis, was wonderful. Belated nomads, tired by the long and dusty march, were slowly moving along. Here and there, tents were being pitched, fires lighted. On the morrow, once more, they would start on their eternal quest. High on the mountain side, broken columns stood in the flaming glory of the setting sun; golden beams danced in the evening haze. And I kept thinking of these Kashkai chieftains, come down from the steppes and highlands of Central Asia, who had grown to love this land and spoke with feeling and pride of the power of Darius and Xerxes.

One morning, the Shiraz radio announced that trouble had broken out in the town. Our quiet life continued, undisturbed by the news. I did not alter my plans. Had I not decided to leave that same evening?

Bibi Khanum, Nasser Khan's mother, had urged me to visit the Tribes in the Beiza district, and spoken with enthusiasm of the beauty of its landscapes. Her firmly expressed wish had overruled her sons' misgivings; they would now do their utmost to help me. Our host, the Persepolis Curator, had offered to take me to Shiraz in his car.

We drove along the shores of a shallow lake, where countless marsh-birds were fishing among the reeds. The rains had been plentiful and the banks were covered with flowers. Climbing into the arid hills that overlook the fertile plain we suddenly dipped into a deep gorge, amid dark cypresses and orange trees; the air was fragrant with the scent of flowers.

Often, in our trips, entering town or village, we had been amused by the slowness and the seeming ineptitude of the police control. Once, even, we had been stopped and delayed, and though our passes indicated that we had permission to travel all over the country, the sentry kept on insisting that this could certainly not apply to his particular district. We had had to wait till a superior officer came to our rescue.

This time the formalities were more elaborate still. All my official papers – and God knows I had quite a collection – were carried off; a soldier jumped on to the running board. In silence, we were taken to the hotel, up till then the symbol and acme of comfort with its shiny bath-rooms, and boiling water galore. But tonight all was silent, dismaying. Police occupied the porter's lodge, a military patrol walked the garden; servants had vanished.

My companion bade me alight and told me that the situation was extremely serious; rioting had broken out; the town was in a turmoil; martial law had been declared; foreigners had been threatened with death, their shops and offices had been burnt, the wine cellars plundered. . .

Here I was, alone on the hotel balcony. Three days ago we were having tea in these charming surroundings, amid the constant coming and going of the various guests. Now, all was silent. From a dark passage a small shy man sallied forth, mumbled a few words of broken English; I remembered him well: he must have been an attendant of sorts. This evening he seemed to be in charge of the abandoned hotel; he took me to my room. A severe storm had broken, and the room was icy. Recalling past delights of warm baths and ample supplies of hot water, I was again disappointed. From the opened tap, only a hissing, gurgling sound issued.

In the vain hope of resuming the journey next day, I called up 'Bagh-è-Aram' on the phone; after several attempts, I finally heard Mohammed's voice. He informed me of the recent happenings: the Americans employed by the 'Point Four Plan' had sought the protection of the Kashkai Chief and had all taken refuge in the 'Bagh-è-Aram'. Their offices had been ransacked, and Mohammed had his hands full; there was no spare mattress or blanket to be found for the night, and next morning he would be faced with the problem of feeding these unexpected guests.

The line was repeatedly cut. He begged me to remain where I was and told me to be without fear.

The enchanting garden was flooded by rain; military patrols walked their beat through the night; the sound of their hobnailed boots on the pavement reminded me disagreeably of war vigils when we might, from one moment to the other, have become the prey of the Gestapo.

The storm had burst as we entered Shiraz, putting an end to rioting, as I learnt later from the newspapers. I read myself to sleep, and when I woke the skies were clear and the breeze fresh and sweet. As if by magic, and as if he had not a care in the world, the Persepolis Curator was sitting in the garden. His news, however, was not pleasant: I had to remain where I was if I wanted to avoid being arrested. He himself had business to attend to, and would call for me in the evening, on his way back to 'Takht-è-Jamshid'. So, once more, I called Mohammed. Being responsible for the Americans, he could not move from 'Bagh-è-Aram'. Would I come over and chat with him? To my regret I had to tell him I thought this would be too difficult. I did not know a word of Persian, I had no car or carriage. How could I, in the present situation and without official papers, cross the town and not be arrested? Weeks later, in the spring camp of the 'Black Mountain', we met again, Mohammed and I. He told me how the Kashkai tribesmen had peacefully occupied the town of Shiraz, restoring quiet and order. He teased me too for having missed this unique show . . . it was all rather infuriating!

My friends had often made fun of my enthusiasm for the beauties of Shiraz; its gardens; its flowers; the fragrance of its wine. That day they were my only solace. During those long, lonely hours, a 'cup of ruby' close by, I whiled away the time, taking photographs of cypresses, roses, lilacs, Josuah trees, and of the amusing reliefs decorating the lower wall of the building, a small palace of the Zend period (eighteenth century).

> Khosrow, king of legend. . .
> Shirin, the beautiful. . .
> whose loves were sung by the poets,
>   and whose tryst was in the distant mountains. . .
> Would I ever reach your land?

THE TRIBES OF IRAN

NATIONS, at the cross-roads, are often trampled upon. Though they are proud of their past, of their history, of their often tremendous contribution to the civilisation of the world, they can but resent being invaded, or treated as mere pawns by the great powers in their struggle for supremacy. These countries either give in and disappear from the map, or else, in times of stress, they will, with all their latent strength, resist these outside influences. Thus, in spite of apparent submission they survive, physically impoverished, morally intact. Friendly, well disposed towards any other nation as long as they are left alone, they resent coercion.

Iran is a land of many problems. Petrol is one, causing envy and intrigue. But there are others. The situation of the country is strategically important; and if the soil is not sufficiently productive, the subsoil is believed to contain many valuable minerals. These, one day, might bring wealth, but in its wake would follow the same intrigues and the well-known procession of greed, graft, and jealousy.

In this country tribes play a large part. They form one third of the population, and could, if properly dealt with, be a stabilising factor, instead of a cause of unrest. True, they are spread all over the country. Peasants used to live in dread of them, for they would swoop down unexpectedly from their hills, plundering and robbing the villages. Though they often avoid the fertile plains, their herds during migration, in spite of precautions, seriously damage the crops.

In succession, the central governments have feared them, and tried to weaken them. Riza Shah Pahlevi not long ago imprisoned their chiefs and had them disbanded. But destruction seems such a negative, wasteful solution to a problem.

Till recently, tribesmen thought mainly in terms of family, of clans, and accepted as a rule a way of life imposed by the climate, the orders of the chief and the welfare of their herds, their main means of livelihood. But wars, and occupation of the country by foreign powers, have now developed a strong patriotic interest in

PLATE 16 A young 'Lord of the Mountains'. Shepherd-boy wearing a typical felt cloak

PLATE 17

The Hafiziyè,
Shiraz
(Page 48)

'Hidden in the
Elburz range
. . . we walked
into peace
and harmony'
(Page 23)

PLATE 18   The 'Il Khan', Nasser Khan, Chief of the Kashkai Tribes (Page 51)

some; and increased the wish for independence and freedom from foreign influences. Usually of proud and ancient races, they have the qualities of the mountaineer. Perfect horsemen, excellent shots, tribesmen are warriors at heart.

They constitute, certainly, a source of unrest in the country. Often at odds with neighbouring tribes, if badly governed or left to themselves they do not hesitate to cross their frontiers in the hope of a fight.

Townsmen get excited and, having lost the need for bravery, will gather artificial courage and boisterousness at meetings, eventually emerging into the streets, where shouting crowds will hold huge parades. But a few well-disciplined patrols, with tanks, will soon disperse the mob, and though the trouble may be serious at the time and liable to recur, it breaks up rapidly.

Countryfolk and mountaineers act differently. They retire into tracts of deserted land, and in the stronghold of hills and forests they bide their time. Accustomed to hunting as a means of livelihood, they are good marksmen and could readily face the prospect of guerilla warfare.

Nomadism is not just an attitude: it corresponds to a geographical necessity. Flocks must graze, and when the grass is burnt dry, they must move to higher pastures. Destroy nomadism, and in a parched and barren country, what is going to replace it? For thousands of years water has been brought down from the mountains and the melting snows, in channels that are dug underground to prevent evaporation. These channels or 'kanat' have to be kept in constant repair, which can only be done by hard and dangerous labour. Irrigation might solve many problems, for when watered the soil is extremely fertile. But so vast a scheme, requiring the investment of huge sums of money, cannot be undertaken without prolonged study.

Loving their freedom and their roving life, nomads are not tempted by the prospect of being forced to settle in mud huts, huddling in dust and dirt. Model villages have been built, but there is need for many more of them.

Poverty means disease; ill-clad and ill-fed vagrants, roaming the countryside and obeying only the laws of nature, will soon fall prey to subversive propaganda. Whereas, well governed, organised, and submitting to a capable and educated chief, they could eventually form semi-nomadic communities, the bare and otherwise useless

E

hills providing pasture for their flocks, the produce of which, in meat, furs, hides and wool, are an important factor in the economic structure of the land.

Riza Shah Pahlevi tried to settle the problem too quickly. It needs ample thought, careful and slow planning, and the advice of experts who have proved their worth by solving similar questions elsewhere.

Uprisings, rebellions, though providing a momentary glow of self-satisfaction, are not solutions in themselves. A wise ruler ought to realise the latent strength of such groups, and, with a certain amount of clever diplomacy, might rally them one after another to his side, instead of letting them fall into decay or under the influence of foreign powers.

Back in Teheran, immersed in the study of the tribes, planning and speculating on possible journeys, I had for a while toyed with the idea of visiting the 'Valley of the Assassins'.

Names cast a spell . . . I had walked one day in the desert, intoxicated by the high mountain air and by five words that beat their rhythm on my brain: 'on the road to Shiraz . . . on the road to Shiraz . . .'

Fascinated by a cup of embossed gold, now in the Teheran Museum, I had already walked up dells shaded by gigantic walnut and chestnut trees, and climbing steep gulleys in burning sun, had looked upon the secluded Kalar Dasht plain. Encircled by high mountains, this was where Riza Shah Pahlevi had wanted to build a retreat in the hills. The cup had been found by workmen who were digging to prepare the site.

Who were these mysterious craftsmen of bygone ages, capable of producing so beautiful a masterpiece? They had lived there, cut off doubtless from the rest of the world by this high mountain barrier. It would have been an ideal spot for an emperors' residence.

Beyond the towering, stately mass of snow covered 'Takht-è-Suleiman', the 'Throne of Solomon', as the Persians aptly name this majestic peak, another ruler had also wished to live, a thousand years ago. 'The Old Man of the Mountain' Hasan-Ibn-Sabbah, built for himself and the sect he had founded, not one, but many castles in the Elburz. When, one hundred and fifty years later, they were destroyed by the Mongols, these castles numbered three hundred and fifty. Hasan-Ibn-Sabbah's henchmen, their followers and descendants, dwelt in those strongholds, drugged and intoxicated by hashish; the 'Hashashin', the 'Assassins' had for a century and a half spread terror in the country, stabbing and murdering; fearless of death; welcoming it, on the contrary, as the means of reaching the promised paradise.

These memories of adventures, these tales of violent deaths, these descriptions of castles perched on rocky pitons, were romantic. It would have been tempting to go there, where so few have recently travelled. But the castles were in ruin, mere fragments in the stony, desert landscape. This was no subject for a film! I needed action, colour, movement.

The Turcoman name conjured up magic pictures: the endless steppe; high grass undulating in eternal winds; galloping nomads; flat-featured men wearing big fur bonnets; jewel-bedecked women; yourts, those round felt tents. But I was unable to go to their country.

I remembered the Kashkai, the beautiful, hieratic, ageless scenes of the migration: herds of goats rushing through stony gulleys like torrents gushing down the mountain slopes; friezes of camels outlined on the rocks.

I had been warned of their fierceness and their love of a fight and plunder. E. G. Browne quotes a conversation with Darcham Bey which illustrates this point: 'The only people that I have seen worse than the Lurs are the Kashka'is' for though the former will usually rob you if they can, and would not hesitate to murder you if you refused to give up your possessions to them, the latter, not content with this, will murder you even if you make no resistance, alleging that the world is well quit of one who is such a coward that he will not fight for his own.' But I had seen their healthy, gay and picturesque throngs. I had seen the Kashkai Chiefs: their mother's eyes spoke of kindness, of friendship. Back to the Tribes then I would go!

SOLO IMPROMPTU

FIVE o'clock in the morning. Sullen and submissive, eyes still heavy with sleep, people clustered around the bus. Its charms and comforts had been lengthily praised. I had been told of its speed, of its excellent springs, and was to learn that all this was partially true. These buses, crammed with passengers, their roofs piled up with luggage, manage to maintain regular hours and a reasonable speed.

I glanced around. Tall Ali Khan was there. At the Kashkai home in Teheran the night before, I had made his acquaintance. Khosrow Khan had detailed Habib, the resourceful, amiable and jovial secretary of the Kashkai family, to organise my impromptu journey. He told me that Ali Khan would see me safely to the camp; but for many good reasons, his job of guardian angel was only to start once we were in Isfahan.

We soon cleared the last suburbs, and while we drove over the road whose curves and bumps were now familiar, I kept thinking of the extraordinary kindness of my two friends. Had it not been for them, I would but have had a glimpse of these regions, and would, undoubtedly, never have returned to that part of the world. I would not have discovered the delights of improvised picnics in incredibly beautiful spots; the long excursions in the deep valleys of the Elburz; the lofty slopes of the Demavend; the charm and peace of the home-coming after days spent in this grand but severe countryside; nor the profound joy and satisfaction of study and of a well finished task.

Wrapped in my old black coat, a dark scarf hiding my hair, I tried to fit into the group of passengers. I did not want to draw attention; I shunned gossip and comments, and feared inquisitiveness. My cameras and films stowed away from curious eyes and fatal dust in bags held on my lap or pushed under the seat, I huddled on the narrow bench and let the hours pass, having, long ago in the East, learnt the art of patience.

Time went by, the engine buzzed and throbbed, we were shaken and bumped around on the endless curves of the road, through a

68

hostile desert of black stones and drab coloured sands. We crawled up the slopes in low gear, catching sight as we topped a rise, of the vast, white and glittering expanse of the salty depression of Kumm.

The dome of Kumm is seen from afar; the town itself is fanatical, hostile to foreigners; the mosque closed to visitors, guarded by severe Mullahs. In the year 816, Fatimè, daughter of the seventh Imam, Musa-al-Kasim, was on her way to meet her brother, the eighth Imam, Ali-al-Riza, when she fell ill and died. She was buried in a Kumm garden, and her family erected a small edifice over her tomb. It was only in the sixteenth century, under the Safawide dynasty, when Shi'ism was proclaimed to be the State religion, that the celebrated sanctuary was built. Shah Abbas II was buried there. Fath-Ali Shah, of the Kajar dynasty, had the cupola gilded, and minarets were a later and not very successful addition. Though a woman, Fatimè was and is held in great reverence, and the sanctuary is the goal of many pilgrims.

Leaving behind us this devout yet ungracious city, we were off again in the desert. A crumbling fire-temple stood guard over the river bed. Further, the horizon was filled by a line of jagged mountains, whose peaks, crags and ridges I had got to know. At a bend of the road the blue tower of an 'Imamzadè' stood out against the dark rocks and the shimmering waters of a stream. We had often stopped there on our way, picnicking in that amazing spot sanctified by this tomb of a holy man.

At regular intervals the bus stopped and the passengers alighted: time for a few moments' rest and a glass of tea. I should have behaved like my neighbours and tried to look like a Persian lady; but the weight of my cameras had stiffened my joints and I had to stretch my legs, walking up and down the highway. As I was ignorant of our time-table, I did not dare wander far towards the villages, and soon returned to the 'caravanserai' or the more modest 'chai-khanè'.

Some of these buildings were quite attractive, built as they were around a pond or a pool.

My companions chatted endlessly together, and kept up a steady stream of jokes that provoked gales of laughter. Cakes and sweetmeats were constantly proffered. I bowed silently and smiled my thanks. But a Persian lady does not travel alone! At our various halts, my odd behaviour had attracted notice. A very young and amiable girl changed seats with my neighbour and tried to start a conversation in hesitant and halting English. 'Who was I? Where was I going? Would I visit her house that same evening, in Isfahan?' From out of the corner of my eye, I watched Ali Khan, seated behind me. Eyebrows raised, looking worried, he placed a finger on his lips . . . silence and discretion were the passwords . . . I murmured that I was studying historical monuments, that I was extremely tired, and with a few mumbled thanks, relapsed into silence.

At last we were in sight of the oasis. It seemed quite near, but I knew this optical illusion, these tricks played by light and distance on the Iranian plateau. Often we had bet on the number of miles that we still had to travel. The pigeon-lofts stood in immense poppy fields, now in full bloom, white flowers nodding in the breeze.

Isfahan, beloved city! But that night I could not walk in the quiet lanes, nor in the 'pools of silence' of the empty courtyards, nor see the golden light reflected in their waters; the sun set or the moon rise above the blue domes.

The bus stopped, and my heart missed a beat. Standing on the steps, a policeman was asking for permits and papers. The men put their hands to their pockets, handed over their documents and spoke, one after the other, probably giving their names and addresses. Would my turn come? No. Was it courtesy or disdain? Women were ignored. I sighed with relief.

There we were, at last, in front of the hotel; amid a great hubbub the luggage was brought down from the car roof. Neatly stowed at the start and protected by a tarpaulin, it was handed to us in a miserable condition. Amongst his belongings Ali Khan had packed some jars of jam. They had broken, of course, and their contents, oozing out, soiled everything else.

The hotel was full and the manager discouraging: one half of the building had been commandeered by the Russian airmen who were fighting the locusts; the other half by the Americans, busy on a similar job. Were they on speaking terms? My question remained unanswered, and I went to look for the home of a kindly French lady who, though herself absent from town, had given me permission to dwell there.

I would have liked to linger here again, for there are few places in the world that I love so well. Was it the ethereal atmosphere? the historical associations? the melancholy beauty of the oasis seen in the twilight as we walked through the deserted graveyards on the lower slopes of the Kuh-è-Sofi? the nostalgic charm of the pines outlined against the blue domes? the graceful buildings? Other cities are beautiful, more imposing even. Few have this appeal.

The intensity of the sky reflecting itself in translucent pools; brilliant and shining cupolas; cool gardens shaded by immense 'chenar', stately cypresses or slender and silvery poplars; all this beauty, made of the essence of things and of man's works of art, is the beauty of Isfahan.

Travellers are fascinated by the monuments built by Shah Abbas. They are not the only ones; others have an equal splendour and charm. One of the most impressive, and the oldest, is Masjid-è-Jum'a, the Friday Mosque 'the most glorious and the most beautiful amongst all mosques' as Ibn-al-Athir's description goes.

I would have liked to go once more to this most venerable sanctuary and watch the colouring of the tiled walls and 'Iwan' change from darkest blue and turquoise to more delicate shades as the sun rose higher above the brick cupola; or wander into the 'Winter Hall', an amazing vaulted room supported by huge square pillars, lit by the pale golden light filtering through alabaster slabs; or study once again the intricate pattern of the elaborate 'Mihrab' that Sultan Uljaitu-Khodabendè had built in 1310. Or I would have gladly spent some leisurely hours in the charming and exquisite courtyard of the Madrasè Mader-è-Shah, the School of Theology, where friendly students greeted us at each visit, offering us cups of tea hastily prepared for us on their small charcoal braziers. Tragic memories haunt this peaceful square, for it was here that Sultan Husain, the last of the Safawide, was murdered in 1722 by the Afghans, during their invasion of Persia.

But that night I had other things to do. Ali Khan had been instructed to find a jeep. I was to be a witness to this transaction: in the shade of the stately 'chenar', planted over three hundred years ago by a royal hand, the machine was brought to a halt. Ali Khan, the driver and a friend alighted and started an argument right in the middle of the town's main avenue, the Chahar Bagh. Throngs of idlers were walking up and down, and we soon became the centre of interest. Angry glances – or, at least I imagined them so – were cast at me. I was annoyed, but rather helpless.

After a long time the bargain was struck.

I slept wonderfully well in the unknown and empty house, and on waking had the joy of seeing the blue dome of the Madrasè Mader-è-Shah framed in the doorway. We were soon on our way, piled up in the jeep. As we left town and though I was seated on the near-side, the policeman took no notice of me, the three men being closely questioned, however. This reminded me of one of Freya Stark's comments: 'The great and almost only comfort about being a woman is that one can always pretend to be more stupid than one is and no one is surprised. When the police stopped our car at Bedrah and enquired where we were staying, the chauffeur, who did not know, told him to ask the lady. "That is no good," said the policeman. "She's a woman."'

My dark clothes and passive attitude were certainly helping me on.

We went at full speed through the desert, heedless of sharp bends and curves, and droves of camels that scattered in all directions as we hurtled by. Passing the town of Shah Riza above which rises the blue cupola of a famous shrine we ran down into the astonishing gap of Yezdikhwast. Since reading Edward Browne's book, *A year among the Persians*, this name had held a fascination for me. Before I ever went to Persia, my imagination travelled on this road, and I had always hoped to see this extraordinary spot.

'My first impressions' wrote Edward Browne, 'were a mixture of disappointment and surprise. On passing the hill I could plainly discern the green dome of a little Imamzadè surrounded by a straggling cemetery: beyond this, apparently on the same level, and situated on the flat plain which we were traversing, appeared the village of Yezdikhwast. Where was its boasted inaccessibility, and sheer precipices which, as all travellers asserted, rendered it one of the most marvellous natural fastnesses to be found in the world? No amount of exaggeration, I thought, could account for such a description of the place I saw before me, which apparently did not enjoy even the most trifling elevation above the surrounding plain. While I was reflecting thus, and wondering if the muleteers had, for some object of their own, deceived me, we passed through the

A shepherd shearing

Breaking camp

cemetery, and all at once came upon one of the most remarkable sights I ever saw.

'Right across our path lay a mighty chasm, looking like the dry bed of some giant river of the past. In the middle of this stood what I can only describe as a long narrow island, with precipitous sides, the summit of which was crowned with tier upon tier of grey, flat-roofed dwellings, which even hung over the edge of the cliff, supported by beams and rafters. These, projecting outwards in all directions, gave to the place the appearance of some strange collection of birds' nests rather than of human habitations. At the upper end this island was almost joined to the northern end of the chasm, the comparatively shallow depression which separated them being spanned by a drawbridge, by raising which all access to the town can be cut off. At all other points a sheer precipice, increasing in height towards the east, protects it from all possibility of invasion. . . Passing over this, we entered a dark passage, which, with occasional outlets into comparatively open spaces, traverses, or rather tunnels through, the whole village, from west to east. This is the only street, for the rock is narrow, though long, and there is not room in most places for more than two houses side by side. My guides informed me that their town, of which they seemed proud in no small degree, was very old – three hundred years older than Isfahan. . .

'As we advanced, the street, at first open above, became entirely covered over by houses, and the darkness was such that we could not see a yard ahead, and were only saved from continual collisions with other passengers by the cries of "Ya Allah" uttered by my companions to give warning of our approach.

'The houses are for the most part three or four stories high, and are entered by stairs communicating directly with the street. On the outer side they are furnished with platforms or balconies, one above the other, which overhang the cliff in a most perilous manner. On to some of these my guides took me that I might admire the view, but my enjoyment of this was somewhat marred by the sense of insecurity with which the very frail appearance of the platforms inspired me. "I should have thought," said I to my guides, "that these platforms would have been very dangerous to your children, for I observe that they are provided with no rail to prevent anyone from falling over." "They are dangerous," was the quite unconcerned reply; "hardly a year passes without two or three falling over and being killed." "I wonder the houses themselves don't fall", I remarked after a brief interval, during which the palpable weakness of the flimsy structure had become more than ever manifest to me. "They do," replied the unmoved villagers.'

This was written over sixty years ago, and the village, though still standing, is crumbling more and more. During a previous journey we had visited some of the ruins, including a small mosque whose walls were badly cracked. Now, everything had fallen in. It is a dismal and sinister place. When I had read about it, it had sounded romantic. Recently, I had seen it often, always with the same wish: to get away as quickly as possible.

The desert was now covered with huge cricket like insects, nearly three inches long. We stopped to look at them. Emerging from every thorny bush, they crawled about on their six spindly legs. Passing cars crushed them; immediately, their next of kin gathered to enjoy the feast! It was all rather disgusting.

We started off again, the driver's friend having taken the wheel with zest. In the East, drivers seem to dislike loneliness and always invite a friend along; it is an amusing custom. I well remember a solitary trip near Calcutta: two handsome hairy Sikh sat on the front seat; one of them drove me around; the other, a rose between his lips contrasting strangely with his neatly rolled beard, held on desperately to an old fashioned horn, honking constantly in the crazy traffic.

We had been told to avoid towns, and particularly Abadè, a city that straggles along the road to Shiraz and is on the border of Kashkai territory, and to drive straight through the desert. Our careless driver, having run out of petrol, headed for the centre of the town and the petrol pump. We had been urged to be discreet. A loud and lengthy argument was started with the pump attendant, just in front of a sleepy and absent-minded policeman. 'Where is the road to Khosrow-Shirin? How long will the drive take? What is the distance?'

Off again, and at break-neck speed on a bumpy desert track that took us west. Slender, tall and pale, the asphodels were in full bloom; the strange big cricket-like insects, whose name sounded something like 'tchak-tchak', crawled over the sands. Holes, bumps and ruts

were cleared at full speed, the driver only slowing down for the
rivers and overflowing ditches that we had to ford. Each time some-
one was sighted, the driver pulled up suddenly, with disagreeable
results: catching us up, the cloud of dust raised by our jeep in-
stantly smothered us! Hailing the passers-by he carried out short but
noisy conversations, then started off again with a jerk.

We passed some villages, closed-in by high walls protecting
them from dust, cattle and thieves alike: then the desert surrounded
us once more.

As we left Abadè, Ali Khan had mentioned 6 'farsakh' (22
miles) the driver 8 or 9. In reality we drove for about 55 miles
before sighting, down below us in a deep ravine, the village of
Khosrow-Shirin, built like a small fortress at the entrance of a vast
and green plain. In the distance lay the Dinar range, its peaks still
covered with snow, its highest summit rising to 17,400 feet.

Another conversation was started. From the shaking of heads,
shrugging of shoulders, gestures, I gathered that Nasser Khan had
not yet arrived in that part of the country. The next day perhaps,
or another. Who could say?

Pretending that, once more, he had run out of petrol, the driver
stated that he would not go further. This, in the land of plenty,
was aggravating and a thin excuse to hide his fear. He did not dare
enter tribal territory, being frightened by the Tribes' reputation of
lust for plunder. Driving us over the last river, clattering noisily
through the village street, he stopped short with a scraping and
screeching of brakes. Pulling out the luggage, he and his friend
carried it into the only shop: typical mixture of a grocer and saddler's
booth. The owner, hearing Nasser Khan's name, bowed to me,
bade me enter, and shook out a carpet in my honour. People collected; soon, in the main house, on the top floor, a room was prepared;
and from the window the village head-man, the 'Ketkhoda' beckoned
to me. He came to fetch me and together we crossed a dark passage,
and a sunlit courtyard where hens were feeding. We climbed steep
and narrow stairs that led on to a freshly swept terrace.

From the room, the 'Bala Khanè' I heard the sound of voices raised
in agitated discussion. Was conscientious Ali Khan trying to
persuade our driver to go on with his job, or was he refusing to pay
him the agreed price? As we left Isfahan, the driver had pushed into

my hand a piece of paper and a pencil, pointing at the same time to the speedometer. I concluded now that if I was supposed to check the distance, I ought also to stop the argument. Climbing down from my room I witnessed prolonged haggling: proffered money was refused; haughty and disdainful gestures emphasised each sentence. Signalling to Ali Khan to cease this discussion, I compromised finally for the very modest sum of 20 Toman.

We were now alone; for the first and only time I started wondering what on earth had made me come to this remote place. Here I was, at a point 560 miles south of Teheran, with no exact notion as to where I was eventually going, nor any idea how we might ever get there. True, Nasser Khan had invited me three weeks ago; but had he ever seriously believed that I would take him at his word? He knew nothing of my more recent plans.

We walked back to 'our' room, Ali Khan and I, escorted by a small and gaping throng, and frowned upon by a very severe Mullah and some of his followers. We sat on the carpet, in an awful draught, and I soon felt that I was going to catch a severe cold. The ride on the bus, the dust, the open windows, had already started fits of sneezing. A tray bearing bread, butter, eggs and the traditional tea-glasses, was set beside us. Breakfast seemed a distant memory. It was now close on two o'clock. I was ravenous. While we ate, a stream of conversation flowed. Repeatedly the name of Nasser Khan was brought up, then suddenly the magic word – lorry. Was that the solution to our problem?

A scribe was ushered in. He sat on the rug, and placing his ink-stand by his side, wrote to Ali Khan's dictation. I was made to understand that a rider, whose horse was tied beneath our window, would be sent with a message to Malek Mansur. By gestures I tried to make Ali Khan realise that we too might ride. To no avail: either there were no other horses in the village, or he did not trust my horsemanship.

His message dictated and his conscience at rest, Ali Khan curled up, drew a blanket around him, covered his face, and in a few moments was snoring peacefully. On the terrace the muttering voices of our hosts, the bubbling of the 'kalyan' (hookah) made a steady background noise.

Solitary, perishingly cold in the awful draught, I tried to find a little warmth in a sun patch that came in through the unglazed window. Spiders had built their nests in the ceiling rafters; I gazed at them patiently, then at the whitewashed walls, and thought of the strange motives that, once in a while, urged me to forsake my garden in Belgium or my clean spotless châlet in the Alps, to roam on distant trails.

Afternoon peace – the sacred siesta hour – had settled on the village. Excepting for the regular snores, the banging to and fro of doors in the breeze, not a sound was to be heard.

When, later, Ali Khan, sighing deeply, opened his eyes, he jumped up in astonishment to see me seated by his side. Then, smiling, he tried to make me understand that we would probably be on the move before nightfall, and pointing to the door, invited me to go out with him. Showing the way, waving his hands, grunting and groaning as if he was leading a camel, preventing me from straying or from taking a wrong turn, he guided me through the village, where the Mullah, still in earnest discussion, threw me scandalised looks, and led me to the green and grassy banks of a delightful river, running and tinkling on stones amid rows of graceful poplars. We climbed a hill. There, on the slope, among the rocks, a pool had formed. From it flowed a spring; lying by it, his face in the water, Ali Khan drank long cooling gulps. I did likewise, enjoying the delicious freshness and the earthy fragrance.

Later, Malek Mansur told me that this was the pool sung by so many poets. Khosrow, the King of Kings, riding past, had seen the lovely Shirin bathing there. Marvelling at her perfect beauty, he fell in love with her and married her. This is how the Persian poet describes this charming scene:

'Tired, the King's horse stopped just where the beautiful Shirin was bathing. Khosrow ordered his pages to wait and to give fodder to the horses. Then, leaving them, he walked forward nonchalantly onto the meadow, going hither and thither on the green grass where flowed a clear spring. . . Looking around on all sides, he suddenly espied a woman as beautiful as the moon, seated like a flower on water the colour of the sky, half-clothed in dark blue satin, combing her hair. As she threw water on her head one would have said that the heavens were showering pearls on the moon. Beholding this entrancing woman, the King's heart was aflame with love, and greatly moved, he wept. Because her hair veiled her eyes, the beautiful woman had not noticed that the king was watching her. But when her face, like a moon, emerged from the dark cloud of her hair, she saw the King. Abashed, she trembled like the moon in the waters of a spring. She could only try to shroud herself in her locks, like the moon in the clouds.'

The story added that Shirin was thought to be of Christian (nestorian) faith. This charming tale, illustrated by countless artists, eventually gave the name of its two heroes to the entire region.

As we walked back toward the village, the sound of a throbbing engine came to our ears. The most enchanting music could not, at that moment, have sounded more pleasant! Was it the lorry? (When in camp, I found out that this particular lorry, at that moment my sole hope, came to the village once a week. Really, I was pretty lucky!) Hearing it, the villagers rushed out; children, in numbers, settled on the walls, ready to watch the show. The lorry rolled along slowly, sedately, swaying painfully from side to side, crossed the river, and stopped in a courtyard. A number of men, carrying bundles, alighted. Ali Khan, the 'Ketkhoda' and several others, hurried towards the driver. This man had met our jeep on the way; its owner had probably borrowed some petrol and had told God knows what kind of a story. The lorry driver seemed neither pleased nor amiable. A violent argument ensued; the words 'benzine', 'backshish' (tip), 'pul' (money), recurred continuously. What was being decided? With a convincing and eloquent gesture, the driver pointed to his cargo of salt. Who was going to unload it? His companion, for he too travelled with a friend on his lonely run, jumped up and started throwing out the heavy yellow blocks, one by one.

I had stood around long enough, so I settled near the children on one of the low walls. By then everybody must have known in the village that I was Nasser Khan's guest. The owner of the courtyard, and of a small house nearby, came and with great politeness bade me take a seat: an iron chair was found, and placed on a carpet right in the centre of the yard. I felt honoured. With pride, he pointed to his family; his wife arrived, carrying a glass of tea, surrounded by her children who, mouths agape, kept staring at me. To thank them for their hospitality and courtesy I dug into a pocket and found there a small toy – I always had a supply of these handy – and gave it to her young daughter who, by a strange coincidence, bore an odd likeness to a photograph of myself when I was three years old.

It was late in the afternoon; the now emptied lorry was swept clean and our luggage was put on board. It was bitterly cold, and it was with pleasure that I donned my old black coat again, though its material was much too flimsy for my taste. We climbed onto the seat – Ali Khan, the driver, his companion and myself. Four men joined our party, and hung onto the sides. As we moved off, I heard again the ominous word 'benzine'. Ali Khan, with quiet assurance, mentioned 6 'farsakh' (22 miles), and looking at the gauge, to my dismay I saw it pointed at 'empty'. Was the needle broken?

There was no track, and the way was marked by stones, occasionally by some very small cairns, or by thorn bushes which had been uprooted and sat on end, but looked to the untrained eye as if they had been rolled and driven by the wind. Our self-appointed guides waved their free hand and shouted; from time to time they jumped from their perch and, running ahead, pushed boulders and rocks out of the way, or tried to find the passage of the fords.

We were heading for the Dinar range, golden in the evening sun; an icy wind was blowing from the snow covered summits.

The lorry pitched and lurched as we drove in low gear. It stuck in marshy ground, backed, started off again with a jerk. Our gay and noisy friends thought all this a great lark, climbed up and down constantly, laughed and joked with the driver, who at times looked earnest and worried.

We passed a small encampment where black tents were pitched and evening fires already burning. The sun was low on the horizon. As it disappeared behind the hills we came to the foot of the range. In front of us, guarded by muddy banks, was a deep river. Surrounded by high cliffs, the ford could not be either crossed or by-passed. The driver stopped short, afraid of getting bogged.

I still hoped against hope: if we all got down and relieved the lorry of this extra weight, we might get it over. Jumping from stone to stone, we scrambled up the further bank; to my dismay I saw the driver, leaving his truck, join our group; at the top of the rise, out of breath, all began an animated discussion. At a run, one of the men set off toward some distant fires, far away in the hills.

The driver had given up, and I certainly could not blame him; for the last two hours we had done all we possibly could to damage his lorry. Had he even sufficient 'benzine' to get back to wherever he came from? Over there, on the bank, on the other side of the stream, the needle of the petrol-gauge still pointed to 'empty'.

It was bitterly cold. To while away the time, Ali Khan lit a thornbush fire; it burnt itself quickly out. The discussion went on. Were we going to spend the night there? Anything seemed possible; and though I was just a little anxious about this chapter of small mishaps, I was enjoying myself thoroughly. Firmly, the driver refused to be paid: He had not been able to fulfil his promise.

It was by now pitch dark, save for the glow of the dying embers. With cocked eyebrow and wrinkled forehead I questioned: 'Nasser Khan?' 'Do farsakh' (8 miles) was Ali Khan's answer. Wagging my fingers in the firelight I showed him that I had decided to walk. What else could we do? The short-lived fire had died out and it was, once more cuttingly cold.

The conversation flared up: the men would take charge of the luggage; Ali Khan shouldered my cameras (at last removed from their bags) and clutching the bundle of newspapers and a biscuit-box he had held on to since Teheran, turned southward. He refused to let me carry anything excepting an electric torch, provided thoughtfully by André.

We set off at a good pace, for Ali Khan had very long legs. I trotted by his side, flashing the lamp on broken ground: stones, pebbles, thornbushes, countless brooklets running down the mountain side. From time to time Ali Khan stopped; his hands being full, I lit his innumerable cigarettes. Stooping, by signs, he would induce me to sit and rest; but I was too cold, and preferred to get on. By match light, we looked at the time: 7.30 – . . . 8 – . . . 8.30 – . . . Ali Khan walked without faltering, certain of the way.

It must have been close on 9.30 when we heard a call, far off ahead. Could it be the shepherds whose fires we saw burning on the hills? Another cry. This time Ali Khan answered. Horses hooves pounded the stones . . . a rider's dark silhouette, outlined in the starlight . . . another rider . . . greetings in the dark . . . explanations. Having received the written message, Malek Mansur had sent horsemen to Khosrow-Shirin; they had been told that we had left

PLATE 19 The 'Il Begh' Malek Mansur, brother of Nasser Khan (Page 51)

PLATE 20 Khosrow, 'King of Legend'. An eighteenth century
relief in Shiraz (Page 63)

PLATE 21   Shirin, 'the beautiful'. An eighteenth century
relief in Shiraz (Page 63)

PLATE 22 Bibi Khanum, 'The Lady' (Page 55)

by lorry. Informed of this, Malek Mansur who well knew that only jeeps can drive over such broken country, had sent parties out to look for us. One group had found us; the others, hearing the shouts, soon gathered around.

Now we were all on horseback; the torch was still burning and lit up the cavalcade. Side by side we rode down the last slopes and arrived at a camp pitched in a protected hollow. Servants, carrying lamps, hurried towards us. The white light of the petrol flames flickered and played on the canvas tents. Nasser Khan and Malek Mansur were much amused by my adventures; they welcomed me with great hospitality. They invited me into a large tent, where next day the guests would be entertained, and where fortunately a charcoal brazier was burning. They told me that the night would be quite cold at this altitude of over 7,000 feet. 'It was going to freeze, so would I keep my coat on?'

Seated on thick carpets we sipped scalding and fragrant tea while the servants brought in trays of food. We ate little but chatted earnestly away, discussing the recent political events. Ali Khan delivered the bundle of newspapers and imparted his version of city gossip.

It was nearly midnight when the two brothers asked me if I was not feeling tired. They escorted me to a tent, and seeing that I had no luggage, Nasser Khan sent for some pyjamas and for his own hot water bottle. O bliss!

F

Part III

THE SPRING CAMP OF KHOSROW-SHIRIN

Where lies thy carpet
There is thine home
PERSIAN PROVERB

LIKE bugle-calls, the neighing of horses and braying of donkeys burst upon my ears. Dawn was breaking. Huddled under my blankets I glanced around with curiosity: on the ground, a lovely carpet; in a corner, a basin and jug of silver metal, filled with water that would be icily cold. I had been too tired and chilled to attempt the slightest effort at cleanliness, the night before. Ashamed of myself, I crawled out of bed and hastily made amends. I was right: the water was at freezing point! My grey sweater and slacks had not been improved by the trip. Who cared? I was too excited to wait for my bags. When would they get there, anyway? Untying the tent flap I stepped outside. I was in an entirely new world! Spread out in a very green plain, the vast encampment was, except on the north-eastern side, hemmed in by barren mountains.

My white canvas tent stood in a group of tents of similar material and colour. Further off were others, blue or ochre, and hidden in the folds of the land, clusters of black ones.

I soon learnt to know the different types: tents made in India, lined with coloured cloth; Persian tents decorated with 'Kalamkar'; this typical hand-printed material with its floral designs was formerly produced in the towns of Isfahan and Kashan. It has been copied in Europe: two monks are supposed to have visited Persia in the seventeenth century and to have brought back with them the carved blocks of wood used for printing; these served as a model in the south of France where the industry is still flourishing in Provence, particularly in the town of Arles.

The more modest and humble tents are made of goat's hair. All have as sole furniture rugs and carpets that vary in quality and design. There are three principal kinds: 'Kali', the beautiful carpets woven on looms; pileless rugs known as 'Gelim'; and the gaily-coloured chequered blankets decorated with tufts of wool called, 'Jajim'.

The camp was astir. Tethered horses, hindlegs hobbled, backs protected by beautifully embroidered blankets adorned with their owners initials or the oriental swastika, strained their necks towards bundles of fresh grass. Countless flocks were on the move and a group of undisciplined and grunting camels was being led to more distant pastures. On the threshold of their tents men sat together, smoking their 'kalyan' and drinking tea. As soon as they caught sight of me, attentive servants hurried forward, carrying a glass bound with silver, and a tray of wheat cakes.

Sitting in front of my tent I enjoyed this wonderful scene. At dawn the colours of earth and sky were incredibly beautiful. The neighbouring tents were still closed; watchful servants stood by. After a while, a tent flap was loosened and Nasser Khan appeared. As he saw me he smiled diffidently and sitting by my side he asked: 'How did you sleep?' In somewhat halting English he explained that, returning from a journey to the south, he had only arrived the night before, a few moments ahead of me. He was here on his brother Malek Mansur's land, and so far his presence was still unknown. This was lucky indeed, for I would be able to spend the entire morning in uninterrupted conversation with the Kashkai Chief.

Hesitatingly at first I questioned him about the tribes, their organisa-tion, their guidance, commenting on the impressions and informa-tion I had gathered. He began by telling me about the recent events in Shiraz: the rioting; the 'Point Four Plan' Americans seeking refuge in his 'Garden of Heaven'; tribesmen arriving in small groups, apparently unarmed and silently filling the city.

A wise chief, he was opposed to trouble and bloodshed, but pointed out that the country was particularly suited for guerilla warfare. He explained by what means news is carried from one part of the territory to another, his orders being taken to the remotest parts by way of mouth in less than twenty-four hours, he assured me. During the recent troubles, the chieftains were kept informed of his wishes and intentions. At a given moment, men by the thousands were ordered to a certain point or district, though they all came from different valleys. He added that for this particular reason I would not see the more spectacular phases and episodes of the migration. Be-cause of political unrest, the men had to remain on their territorial frontiers for fear of disturbances caused by other neighbouring tribes. Less difficult and hazardous routes were chosen so that women and youths, alone, might manage the guidance of the herds.

Slowly, the conversation took a more confidential turn. He re-lated his childhood. His father then ruled the tribes.

'In the days of Kerim Khan Zend (1750-79) one of our ancestors,

Jani Agha, Chief of the Shahlu Tribe, who was said to be a des-
cendant of the Safawide, became a close associate of this sovereign
and acted as his minister. He was rewarded by being appointed "Il
Khan" of what was to become the Kashkai Tribe, a title that can
be translated as "Chief of Chiefs", and is of Mongol origin; it was
probably first borne by Hulagu. When the Kajar ousted the Zend
dynasty, Jani Agha sons were blinded or mutilated.

'The name Kashkai itself, as you have been told by my brother,
may have several meanings and different origins. As we are great
breeders of horses, it would be appropriate if it indicated somebody
whose horse has a white star on the forehead, though "who fled
from the north to the south" could be applied to our Tribes who,
leaving the Caucasus, settled eventually in the Province of Fars.
The name, however, did not appear in any record before the
nineteenth century.

'We ourselves, descendants of Jani Agha, are of the Shahlu Tribe;
this clan is now nearly extinct and comprises only four or five
"houses" or families.

'My father, Sawlat-al-Dawlè, who was the last Il Khan, was also
Military Governor of the Province. In the 1914-18 war, he took
sides against the Allies when they tried to land on the Persian coast
during the Iraq campaign. Later, he was imprisoned by the former
emperor, Riza Shah Pahlevi whose policy was to weaken the tribes,
settle them forcibly and eventually bring about their disappearance.

'My father died in prison, and for six years I shared his captivity.
I also spent some time in exile, in distant towns and provinces. When,
in 1941, Riza Shah Pahlevi was forced to abdicate, I returned to
my Tribes, and ever since, I have ruled them.'

He spoke with admiration of his mother, Bibi Khanum. He
mentioned her love of the Tribes, her undaunted courage.

'While her husband was in prison – though a widow, the mother
of many children,with four sons and two daughters alive; despoiled
of properties and land – she struggled alone to keep the family together; wisely, she sent her younger sons to foreign colleges and
universities. She still gathers them round her, though now she is
seventy years old. Her advice is listened to; her wishes are immediately fulfilled. Deeply loved and respected by all, her kindness to
her people and Tribes is boundless.'

Her name, I was told, is a name of distinction. It is derived of 'Beh-Beh' which means 'brave', 'good', and is attributed to a lady whose qualities are outstanding. The Mother of Christ is known as 'Bibi Myriam', and the wife of Husain as 'Bibi Shehr Banu'... Never given to ladies born and living in the cities, be they even of the aristocracy, it is applied only to those dwelling on the land, wives of local lords, etc.

Nasser Khan talked with pride of the improvements that have been made, of the work of reconstruction that has been undertaken among those who have put their faith in him.

Nasser Khan is not only the arbiter, the judge, and the adviser of the 400,000 men and women of his Tribes. He is also the friendly negotiator who reconciles those who have quarrelled. 'When a quarrel starts' he told me, 'and a quarrel can flare up in the most united families, this dispute must not degenerate into a feud and be carried beyond our frontiers; it must be stopped and the problem solved among ourselves.'

I then questioned him about his authority: 'It must not be contested or discussed', he answered. 'Should I feel that, among all my men, five only were against me, I would abdicate without any delay. My role of Chief must be played with the agreement and help of all.'

During the following days, I often witnessed long discussions between Nasser Khan and his visitors. He does not consider himself omnipotent or infallible, but before making up his mind and coming to a decision, will listen attentively to different opinions. He consults his chieftains, but will also when necessary, seek the advice of the most humble shepherds. These are not shy: looking at him frankly and steadily, they give their ideas on matters which concern them.

The function of Chief is not exclusively hereditary. Normally the eldest son succeeds his father; but he will first have to prove that he has the required moral qualities as well as the physical strength and endurance that will render him worthy of bearing the title of 'Chief of Chiefs'. When they address Nasser Khan, or speak of him, the tribesmen never give him any other name than that of 'Il Khan'. His brother, who acts as his right hand, bears the title of 'Il Begh', but oddly enough, should Nasser Khan be away, the brother or member of the family who temporarily takes his place will be given the name of 'Il Khan', showing, in this way, that it is he who has the power and the authority for the time being.

If ever the Chief proved himself unworthy of the Tribes' trust, he would be requested to retire and let another become ruler in his stead. In that case, he would still be treated with respect and affection, but one would no longer be pledged to obey him.

The Kashkai are proud and conscious of their superiority when they compare themselves with other tribes. Fiercely independent, they love their hills, their rocky defiles, their grassy slopes, where there are no roads but only difficult trails, knowing that this country has always been a protection against invaders.

Nasser Khan admires the qualities of the various Western powers, and has many friends among them. Well informed on contemporary questions, he is an ardent nationalist and would like to see Iran's problems solved to the benefit of the Iranian people. Russian influence must not be discounted, for there is a natural bond among Asiatic countries and communities; but communist theories are in direct contradiction with the Kashkai Tribes' aspirations and ideals. So communism is feared.

Actually, Nasser Khan is against any form of violent action that might cause military intervention. This would only lead to more internal agitation and would in the end favour the communists. Knowing by experience the tragedy of troubled times, the impermanence of circumstances and of human endeavour, his main thoughts are for his own tribesfolk and their welfare.

The Kashkai are always willing to help each other, he told me, adding the following tale which had a biblical flavour. Recently one of the tribesmen sustained a great loss; a storm broke and part of his flock was killed by lightning. His friends and neighbours got together; each one brought a present: one carried a lamb; another a young kid; others led a goat or a sheep. When, after a while, he counted his herd again, he was surprised to see that, instead of dwindling, through the kindness and comradeship of the Tribe it had considerably increased.

At their origin, the Kashkai Tribes were forty-four in number; each Tribe has its own chief, the 'Kalantar' and a number of 'Ketkhoda' or head-men. Under them again, and having less authority, are leaders of groups called 'Rish-è-Safid' literally 'white-beards'.

One of these clans, alone, obeys the Il Khan directly and has no 'Kalantar'; it is the Tribe of the Amalè, from which is chosen Nasser Khan's bodyguard. This Tribe numbers about 45,000 people. These men are the Khan's escort and also his executive power. Nasser Khan is extremely proud of these youths, of their hunting prowess and of their valour as warriors. He told me that the education of all the young boys, born in the tents and brought up in camp, is a problem to which he gives great attention. In the towns and villages inhabited by semi-nomadic Kashkai, not far from the migration routes, schools exist or are being built; the tribal children are sent to attend them. Holidays are spent in camp so as to develop or maintain the love of nomadic life. When this taste is firmly rooted and when the youth's education is ended, if he has shown special aptitude for study he will be sent, often at the Chief's expense, to a high-school or university, in Isfahan or Teheran, for instance, or even abroad in Europe or America. Thus the Il Khan's brothers studied in Germany, England and France. His eldest son passed examinations in French in Lausanne, and is at present continuing his medical studies in America in the hope of being, later on, of use to his people.

Nasser Khan, who has two sons and four daughters, showed me then a photograph of his eldest son Abdullah. This photograph was carefully kept in the folds of his pocket-book.

Though of slenderer build than his father, Abdullah seems to have the figure of a perfect horseman. I was told later of some of his accomplishments. Large, dark, eager eyes, beautifully designed, thick, black eyebrows, a sensitive smile, and a humorous, mobile expression, were the characteristics that struck me when I looked at his picture.

The problem of the migration preoccupies the Il Khan. It is he who decides and plans it: he indicates the roads to be followed, the date of departure, the different grazing lands, the length of the stay in the various camping grounds. Nasser Khan, however, fears that the introduction of modern appliances and facilities may soon corrupt the independent spirit of the nomads who will gradually lose their taste for this hard and free existence. Because of the excellent profit made by cattle raising and by farming – and a number of Kashkai are only semi-nomadic and, being good farmers, produce enough corn and food for the entire district – he believes that, little by little, his people will be tempted to become sedentary. To help them settle when necessary, he advises them, and buys land for them which they can cultivate. Since his return to his Tribes more than twelve years ago, out of love and interest for his people, he has voluntarily distributed to those in need part of his own properties.

As I was questioning him, the Il Khan listened attentively. Head to one side, eyelids lowered, a hovering smile softening his rather severe countenance, he pondered each question at leisure. I told him how deeply the noble sight of the migrating Tribes had moved me.

'It is our life', was his reply. 'Unchanged for thousands of years. We love it, and do not fear it, though it is sometimes adventurous and uncertain. Children are born on the way . . . we do our best to improve sanitary conditions and to relieve the sick. We have organised modern transportation and, when possible, the ailing are carried to the town hospitals. But our life is hard, and death finds us here or there. The Mongols have already commented on it: "Must not those who are born in a tent meet death in a battle?" – My ancestors all met it suddenly and violently. We do not fear death by the road-side! Sometimes, one of our brave warriors' or hunters' last wish is to be buried near our mountain tracks, so that future generations, passing near his tomb, will dedicate a pious thought to his memory.'

While he was talking, I suddenly remembered one of those country burial-grounds on the road to Firuzabad; from afar, it looked like a part of the desert. The only difference was that a few stones stood out, casting a shadow on the sands. I was strangely attracted to these sad yet peaceful sites, which have an ethereal and serene appeal in the immensity, the eternal beauty of the Persian landscape. During long, meditative wanderings in the cemeteries that lie at the foot of the jagged Kuh-è-Sofi, near Isfahan, or the small Armenian grave-yard on the first slopes of the Elburz, the melancholy rhythm of Sa'adi's verse had impressed itself on my mind: 'Have no attachment to this world of illusion. . .' Usually the Muslim stones carry just a plain inscription. Here, in this small piece of soil, some were ornate, others very simple, and we had been fascinated to find, so close to the nomads' trail, tombstones decorated with crudely cut figures of horsemen.

Nasser Khan was astonished by my way of travelling alone. He wanted to know why I had wished to visit his Tribes. I told him that, having heard through friends of the beauty of the migration, I had wanted to see it. Accustomed as he is, to living with the nomads, this did not entirely satisfy him. In his turn he questioned me, wondering what made me, from time to time forsake my home and my children to undertake difficult journeys in distant lands. Feeling that his sympathy was more than idle curiosity, seeing that his eyes were kind and thoughtful, I told him that I too, had met loneliness and sadness. In a land where all love poetry, and many are poets in their way, I quoted the lines of Hafiz:

> Light of mine eyes and harvest of my heart,
> And mine at least in changeless memory!
> Ah! When he found it easy to depart,
> He left the harder pilgrimage to me!

Nasser Khan then said to me: 'From different, distant countries I have had requests to make a film depicting the life and customs of my Tribes. I was offered large sums of money for this. But our customs are not for sale! You, Madame, have asked for nothing. You have travelled thousands of miles in the sole hope of seeing and recording something that is moving, beautiful. Madame, my Tribes are at your service. Do as you please.'

The sun was high in the sky and we sought shelter from its burning rays beneath the tent flap. Watchful servants, at regular intervals, brought us glasses of fragrant tea. Around us, people silently busied themselves with their daily tasks; young shepherds played quietly near their flocks. The beauty of this ancestral scene, of the fertile grassy plain framed by austere bare mountains, impressed itself on my memory. . . This had been going on for thousands of years, since the beginning of time. . . Would man, in his anxious quest for improvement, destroy this idyllic, biblical life?

In Firuzabad, Nasser Khan had proudly shown us a group of women, clad in flowing skirts, at work on a carpet that one day would be the sole ornament of the Chief's tent. We now discussed the beauty of the Kashkai rugs and the art of weaving. Their designs are characteristic; some are geometrical; others have distinctive patterns, easy to recognise, though the origin is lost in the hazy past, and it is difficult to know if they are inspired by familiar animals: fish, turtles, or the stretched lambskin, symbol of fortune?

I had read that, in Persia it is admitted that the cleanest, healthiest, most prosperous and orderly tribes produce the best rugs. The Kashkai, who are one of the most advanced tribes of Fars, are considered the best weavers. Their rugs are known as Turki Shirazi. Though rug weaving is not solely a commercial proposition, the output on the market of Shiraz is important. 'But', added Nasser Khan, 'our women are very proud of their rugs. They wash, spin and dye the wool with great care. They weave on horizontal looms set a few inches from the ground. When they change camp, following their herds and flocks, the loom is taken up and reset. This moving of the loom causes irregularities in the weaving, which are typical of most tribal rugs. Our most beautiful and valuable rugs are kept in the Kashkai tents, or handed out as gifts for weddings and feasts.' Pointing to a group of men who were carrying an enormous carpet into the reception tent, he explained that a rug of this size would take eight women about two years to finish; 'there is little doubt,' he said, 'that the art of weaving will soon be industrialised and will lose its beauty.' So far the Kashkai have maintained its tradition and quality. The colour of the rugs, as well as those of blankets and saddle bags are of vivid tones, and are noted for their bright yellows and cheerful reds. The borders are worked in various hues and the edges are often decorated with tufts of gay wools. The best and most elaborate carpets are woven, naturally, in the less mobile encampments, and the most famous weavers are the Kashkuli and the Shesh Boluki Tribes.

For generations the Kashkais have kept secret their knowledge of the plants and mountain herbs which give to their carpets their particularly brilliant tones. Sending for a very old woman – tiny, her face covered with wrinkles, parched and tanned by the dry mountain air – he told me that she was one of the few who preserved this mysterious science. Gathering and picking the herbs in deep forests or on hills, she brews them in big cauldrons and mixes them with skill, producing the fast colours that give to these rugs their beauty, their value and their great reputation. Before leaving this world for everlasting green pastures, she will hand on these precious recipes to those who must follow her.

Later in the afternoon, I watched her as, squatting in front of her tent, looking like an aged sorceress in a fairy-tale, she stirred up her fires and tended the steaming brew of the 'Kaveshk', the plant that yields the beautiful yellow colour.

By mid-day the heat was intense; we abandoned my rug and sought the deep shade of the reception tent where lunch was soon served: creamed soup, flavoured with mountain herbs; dishes of rice, roasted mutton, stewed vegetables, dates, bowls of sour milk.

The hottest hours of the day were hours of rest; silence pervaded the camp. In the open the glare was unbearably strong, and the semi-darkness of my tent very welcome. Squatting on the carpet, leaning on my mattress and a pile of cushions, I jotted down notes and tried to get the dust out of my cameras and lenses.

Through the opening, far away in the distance I could see horsemen, skirting the hills and riding towards camp. They had started at dawn for Khosrow-Shirin and were returning, carrying across their saddles the luggage we had left behind. My bags were somewhat the worse for wear, and when I had unpacked them, were taken away to be repaired. As the day waned, the light softened once more, so I started out to study the prospects for photographing. Immediately, I was surrounded by a crowd of inquisitive yet polite and respectful children who became my constant companions during all my strolls.

Though Nasser Khan had told me that here he was on his brother's land, I soon realised that he alone gave orders. I would have to ask his help: as soon as they saw me, people stopped and gazed, then seeing that I was carrying a camera, and knowing nothing of the principles of motion-picture making, they one and all 'froze', posing in stiff and silly attitudes. This would never do. It had already, in other parts of the country, spoilt for me countless yards of film. So Nasser Khan's instructions went out, and were dutifully followed.

In the twilight and the coolness of the evening, the camp came to life again; this was, for the Kashkai, the sacred hour, the hour of the horse-parade. The Kashkai are, first and foremost, horse-breeders. The Chief and his guests gathered in the reception tent, while tea was served once more. The grooms untethered the horses. Still protected by their beautiful blankets, they were mounted, their riders parading them up and down and putting them through their paces. Foals followed the mares as the horsemen circled the tents, making a very pretty picture.

Gradually, peace settled on the plain of Khosrow-Shirin; the evening fires were lit. I joined Nasser Khan and his brother, alone now under the tent. Nasser Khan was engrossed in the study and perusal of messages that he had received; calling for his writing-pad, and placing it on his knees, he started writing. Seated near the brazier, Malek Mansur and I chatted away. I had donned my 'pustine' the comfortable local coat made of lambskin. The wool is worn inside; the hide, tanned a yellow colour, is fancifully embroidered. This garment is extremely warm, and I kept it on through the evening and all through the night. It must have frozen again, for the cold crept in under the canvas, and chilled the ground.

The points and merits of the parading horses were now discussed with me. The Kashkai horses are thoroughbreds; Malek Mansur proudly told me that his stallions had pedigrees dating back four hundred years; he considers them invaluable. When I asked him if he would sell them he exclaimed, horrified: 'Never would we think of selling these horses . . . occasionally, to honour a special friend, we might offer him one as a gift. But would we sell our wives or our sisters?' . . . He told me also that, to improve their stock, they sometimes bought horses in Khuzistan.

Malek Mansur spoke of his horses with love, and even with tenderness. 'The horses share their master's life, tethered in front of his tent. When a mare is foaling, she shelters within it. They play a part in every feast: a cavalcade rides out to fetch the bride. And groups of caparisoned but riderless horses are led to the burial ground and stand in a circle around the tomb during funeral ceremonies'.

To create a friendly atmosphere, I had in Firuzabad related tales of our hunting trips in the Rocky Mountains and on the Norwegian moors. Realising that I had some knowledge of this sport, Malek Mansur told me that he had organised, in my honour and so that I might film it, a hunt in the hills. He then went off into detailed descriptions of his life in the open. When he is not with the Tribes, he is in the mountains or deep in the forests. He talked of these with wonder and admiration. This was surprising: for the first time, I had found somebody in the East who had respect for trees and shrubs. Usually, Muslim territories have a stripped, barren aspect:

trees have been always cut down, never replanted; goats and sheep have nibbled all the vegetation. On the shores of the Caspian Sea even, the forests, though dense, are pitiful to see; the trees, their branches lopped off by charcoal burners, stand gaunt and immense, like mutilated giants. In Kashkai territory we had noticed the wooded slopes; true the trees are rather stunted, but Malek Mansur assured me that beyond the range, towards the south, are oak forests that can bear comparison with those of Europe. He said that the Kashkai wage war on those who plunder their forests.

The hours passed as we chatted. I was getting accustomed to squatting on a rug and soon had no more need for the big roll of bedding – made of my mattress and embroidered blankets – that Nasser Khan's servant pushed against my back each time I moved. The white glare of the petrol lamp threw dancing shadows onto the canvas; the evening meal was carried in, each dish being set on the carpet in unvaried order. These immense quantities of rice and meat were impressive. It is customary for the Il Khan to offer food to all his visitors. The dishes are first brought to his tent; when he and his guests are served, they are then carried out to the followers and attendants.

Nasser Khan is extremely frugal. In the evening he scarcely ate at all, and seemed to sustain himself on numerous glasses of sweet tea. I never saw him smoke or drink wine or spirits. Before taking his leave and retiring, Nasser Khan asked me to be up early. We would all ride out together in search of game.

That night it was bitterly cold again. It is an extreme climate: at noon the sun was scorching; at night, the water in the silver mug by my bed was covered with a coating of ice. I rolled myself up in the warmest things I could find. Nasser Khan's pyjamas were ample; under them I put on layers of sweaters and woollies; to top off this odd get-up, I pulled on the heavenly 'pustine'. Its smell, I must admit, was strong, rather like Irish Stew; but what did that matter? In spite of all these precautions the icy cold seeped up from the bare soil.

Next morning the entire camp was on the move: sheep were being driven towards Nasser Khan who, interested, stood in the centre of a group, inspecting the passing flocks. Nasser Khan is greatly

PLATE 23   High mountains on the road to Kalar Dasht   (Page 66)

PLATE 24   'Carved high on the cliffs' The first Sasanian
rock-carving (Page 58)

Ali Khan, my guide
(Page 68)

'Showing us the young lambs born that very day' (Page 43)

PLATE 26   The Elburz Range. In the distance, to the extreme right,
the Demavend   (Page 68)

interested in the welfare of all these animals; he is teaching his people modern methods. The help of the Veterinary Institute of Hesarek has been sought, and while I was in camp I saw Persian delegates of the Point Four Plan, come to inoculate the sheep. These splendid herds are the fortune of the Tribes. The sheep, of pure Turkish breed, are larger, stronger, and fatter than those of other parts. They also carry the big, heavy appendage that has given them the name of 'broadtail'.

It was shearing time. In a sheltered nook behind our tents, men were already at work. The animal was seized, thrown onto its back; its legs were tied with rope. A few deft strokes of enormous sharp shears removed the fleece; like a discarded garment, it lay on the ground. The sheep picked itself up and gambolled, glad to be free again; then suddenly, and as if ashamed of its nakedness, stopped.

I lingered near these groups. The young men gathered around Nasser Khan were of the Amalè Tribe, whose name means that they are at the service of the Il Khan and of his chieftains: they prefer the European style of dress now, and often buy practical but unbecoming clothes at some allied army dump. This is, to my mind, a great pity: the Kashkai cloak was most elegant; sometimes of brilliant colours, though often grey; it was long, slashed at the sides and sleeves, and caught at the waist by an ample sash. The trousers are often baggy, perfect in shape for those who spend long hours in the saddle or sitting crossed-legged on the ground. In Persepolis I had noticed that Darius' warriors, the Medes depicted on the famous reliefs, wore, probably for the same reason, exactly the same type of clothing.

All the Kashkai men and boys wear the typical headdress; it used to be a round felt cap; now, since the rule of Nasser Khan, it is a modern version of an ancient model – a brown or grey felt hat, with rather high crown and turned up side-flaps, that, according to the angle at which the hat is set and the way the flaps are bent, can shelter them from sun and rain, or protect their ears from the biting cold. Worn smartly, even rakishly, it enhances the gaunt, handsome faces. This hat is the tribal sign of distinction. Ali Khan carried his carefully wrapped all the way from Teheran. As soon as he neared tribal territory, he set it on his head. In earnest discussion in the centre of this group, Nasser Khan stood bareheaded. Alone in the camp,

G

both he and Malek Mansur never wore the hat, except when on horseback. Now he was giving instructions to his followers; some men left, rode away, then returned a few moments later.

This morning they all looked ready for a military expedition; they had shouldered their guns; on their chests or waists were cartridge belts. While I was filming, tea was brought to me where I stood and it was signified to me that I should hurry. People were restless; they came and went, horses were led to and fro; they tossed their heads, shaking their flowing manes, champing their bridles as they stamped and pawed the ground. Nasser Khan walked towards me. He knew, for I had told him, that I had a weak back; also that I must carry cameras and equipment; thoughtfully he had provided a mule and requested me to ride it. For choice, I would have preferred a prancing arab – and doubtless run into plenty of trouble. His suggestion was wise, though it humbled my pride.

Several men were detailed to ride with me, and I saw that Ali Khan was among them. He immediately took charge of my tripod and we started off, heading a cavalcade that increased as we went. For a while, Nasser Khan and Malek Mansur rode on either side of my mule, chatting and explaining their hunting tactics, pointing to the places where I should take up my position.

This cavalcade of armed men was impressive; they numbered about two hundred. Looking at them as they rode through rocky gullies I thought once more of Persian miniatures depicting princely hunting parties, though their grey or khaki clothes made me bitterly regret the flowing, coloured coats of old. The horsemen cantered off; for the first time I saw Nasser Khan, astride his white horse, wearing the Kashkai hat, the tribal emblem.

A small group had ridden ahead and was now scouring the mountainside in search of game. This expedition was only a sham hunt, organised so that I might film the horsemen. It was spring and the Kashkai are respectful of the laws of nature. Still, they wanted to give me a chance of recording their favourite sport.

During this outflanking manœuvre I had time to catch up with Malek Mansur and to film him as he was riding along, his hawk on his fist. Nasser Khan and the other riders had disappeared behind high rocks. Malek Mansur told me that, contrary to European customs, the hawk is caught young, trained in a few weeks, and let loose again as soon as the hunting season is over. This one, a goshawk, had been caught quite recently and looked fiercely at me with its beady, yellow eyes.

He dismounted to talk to me. He was holding his horse's bridle and carrying the bird when somebody cried out, pointing to a hare running up the mountain, far away, seemingly out of reach. Its fur blending into the colours of the landscape, it was barely visible save for the spouts of dust it kicked up as it fled. Malek Mansur seized the gun his attendant was holding; kneeling, he aimed, fired. In the distance, the hare rolled over. A rider galloped off and carried it back, messy, bloody and shaken by convulsive movements.

I asked Malek Mansur if his aim was always as accurate? Leaning on his horse as on the shoulder of a friend, he laughed back at me: 'Why, of course! . . . If I see, I kill. . . . If I don't see, I don't shoot! . . .'

The hunters had now climbed to the top of the rocks. I could see Nasser Khan's silhouette, outlined on the sky, and the men running nimbly, in very broken ground, jumping from rock to rock. Here again, I was reminded of landscapes painted by miniaturists; those artists in no way exaggerated the nooks and crannies and towering cliffs.

This time, the hunters flushed a partridge. It rose and flew off, gliding towards some rocks, and hid in a cleft between boulders. As this hunt had been organised for the sole purpose of my film, the bird was immediately routed out. The hawk was let loose. With its talons and sharp beak it set upon the poor bird. The scene was so cruel that one of the men put an end to it by cutting the fowl's throat. As I now had an ample harvest of pictures, the hunt ended, for this was the month of May, the birds were nesting, and the Kashkai wished to protect the game.

In spite of the very rough going, these tribesmen always hunt on horseback. They are remarkable riders and shoot usually from the saddle as they gallop. When on foot in the mountains, they are extraordinarily quick and sure-footed, running over the rocks at incredible speed.

In the evening, in the shelter of the tent, Malek Mansur called for his papers and showed me photographs of some of his shooting expeditions: five wolves, side by side, killed in one morning; four mountain sheep with huge winding horns; lovely ibex whose immense antlers curved and spiralled gracefully... Sitting near the brazier, nursing a painful rheumatic arm, his face lit by the glowing embers he told me tales of fighting and of valour, of skirmishes and battles in which he, as a youth, had played a part.

Having read stories of the Mongols, of Jenyhis Khan's warriors, I was reminded of similar tactics: 'In the daylight watch with the vigilance of a wolf, at night with the eyes of the raven; during battle, like a hawk sweep down on your prey', is an old saying. Describing the Mongols, the monk Jean de Plan Carpin had written in the thirteenth century: 'As soon as they espy the enemy, they charge them, and each one lets fly three or four arrows. If they realise they cannot break them up, they withdraw towards their own men, in order to be pursued and so draw the enemy into an ambush. If they realise that the enemy is stronger, they remove themselves to a distance of one or two days' march, and plunder the neighbouring districts . . . or else they camp in a well-chosen site and when the enemy starts to make off, they reappear unexpectedly.'

It is certain that these tribesmen owe to inherited habits and customs much of their ability to manœuvre in difficult country. As their ancestors did, they wait patiently for stag and deer to wander down from mountain slopes towards the drinking places, or drive game, beating up bushes and marshy plains, encircling the fleeing animals.

A great number of young men had gathered around Nasser Khan to take part in the morning's sport; now all in the neighbourhood knew that the Ill Khan was in the district, so in the afternoon visitors came from their different valleys to call on him. Riding up to the camp, they tethered their horses near the first tents; then, respectfully, approached on foot. The elders, often chieftains of subtribes or clans, walked ahead. Hands folded on their breast, they bowed deeply in front of the Chief and for a moment remained standing, in silence, then sat in front of him, crossed-legged or squatting on their heels. Their sons or followers, carrying in their arms, as tribute, young kids or lambs, bowed in their turn, presenting their offerings. The poor bleating animals were immediately passed on to attendants. Their throats were soon cut; later in the day, they reappeared in the guise of delicious roasted 'kebab'. Meanwhile, unless they were expressly invited to share the feast, the young men remained standing in respectful attitudes, sometimes for hours.

Nasser Khan has progressive ideas about the welfare of his people. Abstemious, frugal, sleeping but little, carefully yet simply dressed – In Firuzabad, a dark suit – in camp, a tweed jacket – he knows the moral strength of self discipline. Exacting in regard to himself, he has the greatest respect for tradition; he wishes to convince the younger generation of its importance and value, and of the necessity for implicit obedience to authority.

As if to emphasise this point, he invited that evening a number of the 'Amalè'; while Malek Mansur and I looked on, he handed them some presents, prizes for recent deeds. The fact of my being a Belgian had awakened the interest of all these hunters. Had I not come from the country where famous fire-arms are made? Journeying in Belgium, the Kashkai Chiefs had visited the celebrated Fabrique Nationale, and now they showed me their treasured possessions; some of these guns were going to be the reward of those who, during the troubled days in Shiraz, had shown initiative and zeal. This town, on the limits of Kashkai territory, is always influenced by tribal policy; the recent riots had been quelled, law and order reestablished by the rapid and pacific intervention of the Tribes. Leaving us in Firuzabad, Nasser Khan had travelled south and meeting his various chieftains had notified them of the necessity of occupying the town. Thousands of men, apparently unarmed, slipped into the city, and their presence alone was sufficient to restore calm.

Now the precious guns were brought to Nasser Khan who, with a few words, handed them to those he wished to thank and to reward. Bowing deeply, the men took their gifts and left the tent. This was no doubt their custom, though I was astonished to see that so valuable a present was received without a word of acknowledgment; but does the soldier thank the general who decorates him? He stands to attention and salutes!

Malek Mansur told me that these rewards were considered to be the supreme mark of esteem. I then asked him if, in case of disobedience, there would be some form of punishment? He replied by telling me the following story: A group of men had been ordered to join up Shiraz at an appointed hour. On the way they had encountered very rough going and, delayed by a severe hail storm, had been forced to seek shelter. Consequently, they were late in arriving. Nasser Khan, who organises every phase of the migration, decided that these men would be deprived for one season of their accustomed and excellent pasture-lands, and would be sent, instead, to less favourable grazing grounds. This severe punishment was considered absolutely fair and was accepted without a murmur. 'Those who are under the Chief's orders must know neither rain nor snow, nor storm, but must obey his word.'

Incidentally, this group of men was among our party; their smiling faces and constant joking proved that they bore no ill will. Malek Mansur added that their behaviour had been so good that he would intervene and ask his brother to shorten their penance.

This spirit of equality, comradeship, and brotherhood amongst the Kashkai, is particularly noticeable. They often intermarry and are therefore nearly all related to each other.

Many children played around the camp; one very young horseman galloped ceaselessly about, dressed in a fancy suit made of black, red and white chequered material. Malek Mansur's young daughter, carefully escorted by an aged attendant, prowled near my tent in the hope of receiving a toy. To coax shy children and prevent them from running into hiding, I always carried with me a supply of small playthings. My store held out till the end of my stay. On the last evening I shared out the contents of my bag among the young shepherds who had followed me during my strolls; as they walked away, awed by these unexpected – and very modest – gifts, and solemnly trying out some celluloid flutes, their notes sounded fragile yet familiar in the vast expanse of the Persian plateau.

Up to now, the camp had seemed void of women. In the distance I had caught glimpses of bright dresses, but my appearance had always caused these timid ladies to retire. I knew Nasser Khan's wife to be in California with her children who are studying there. But where was Malek Mansur's wife, the mother of the pretty little girl? He told me that she had been ailing, yet would greet me on the morrow. She was obliged to show herself at last. The elders had come to say that we must be off: the flocks were rested; damage caused by recent rains to clothing and tents, repaired. The grass had to be spared, so that other herds might follow us in a few days time on the yearly trek to the highlands and summer camp of Semiran.

A feeling of excitement pervaded the camp; it was even more acute then on the previous morning. As I stepped out in the golden rays of dawn, attendants were already at work. On all sides people were methodically busy: tents were folded, their props, big wooden poles, piled up in stacks. Where yesterday the sheep were being fleeced, bags were gathered together, camels loaded. Everything might have been confusion, disorder. But each man knew his part and worked quickly, efficiently, accustomed to routine.

This was indeed a spectacular sight. Hobbled camels, one leg bent and tied at the knee, jumped clumsily around; others made to kneel, growled with impatience while heavy bags were lifted on to their backs: folded rugs and carpets were being strapped over the loads. I could have watched all this for hours.

The women, so shy up to that moment, were now extremely active. Still dressed in their magnificent skirts and bodices, they were even more energetic than the men, running from one load to another, lifting enormous bundles and heavy packs. Malek Mansur's wife, a most elegant figure, rode in a green velvet coatee and beautifully embroidered white tulle skirt worn over numerous and ample petticoats.

Though Nasser Khan's tent was still closed, his attendants, one carrying his hat, were standing guard at its entrance; a servant was dispatched to me and signalled that I must hurry. I had been so busy that I had even forgotten my tea. It was carried out to my mule, and while cameras and tripod were being hoisted, I swallowed it at a gulp.

We were off. I was leaving forever this peaceful, heavenly valley. Nasser Khan joined me; trotting by my side he explained that he had organised everything so as to make my task easy. However, there was not a moment to lose. He would be able to control the speed of his horsemen, but once they had started, the huge wave of camels, donkeys, goats, cows and sheep, would be on its way, sweeping over me. It was up to me to find a vantage point; and once there, I would not be able to move in this overwhelming tide of men and animals. He enjoined me to be careful and warned me that I might easily be knocked down and trampled.

Malek Mansur stayed beside me and was a great help: through the sights of my camera it is difficult to see details, so from the saddle he shouted useful information:

'Nasser Khan has started; we can still hold him back; are you ready?'

'I am.'

A rider was sent to say that we were all set, and Nasser Khan rode forth leading his men. From afar, surrounded by such a multitude, astride his white horse, he reminded me of pictures of Napoleon, at the head of his staff. . .

They trotted by quickly.

Reloading my camera, I was back at work:

'Look out, a fine group of horses. Beware, don't stand too close.' Malek Mansur shouted as a herd of camels charged straight towards me. But this was just the kind of shot I wanted, so I held my ground praying that the tripod would not be knocked over. Clouds and swirls of dust, lifted by the passing animals, covered this weird spectacle with a thickening haze.

This was the greatest and most solemn moment of the migration. At a quickening pace the horde poured over the rocky slopes of the mountain. Soon it would find peace and the enchantment of vast grazing-lands covered with golden flowers; rivers flowing in abundance; gushing springs, and clear waters reflecting the eternal blue sky.

The camels were already unloaded as I rode up to the new encampment; Nasser Khan's tent was pitched, protecting us from the morning sun. As if by magic, tea was ready. The day's march was over; people were smiling, relaxed. All now was quiet, peaceful . . . such must have been the feelings of the Tribes of Israel, arriving in the Promised Land. The camp was quickly organised. From all sides mallet blows could be heard, as the tent pegs were driven into the ground. One by one the tents were erected; carpets and rugs, dusty from the treck, were beaten, shaken out, or dragged on the fresh grass; guns and precious rifles laid with care on blankets. Bundles of all kinds, coloured and embroidered bags were lying around. In a group, apart from the crowd, the women had gone into seclusion, busying themselves with the luggage.

PLATE 27   Pool of a 'caravanserai' on the road to Kumm   (Page 69)

PLATE 28   Yezdikhwast, on the road to Shiraz   (Page 72)

PLATE 29   'The village of Khosrow-Shirin, built like a small fortress'
In the distance, the Dinar range (Page 75)

PLATE 30   Flocks grazing at the camp of Khosrow-Shirin (Page 85)

Up till then I had only seen one large reception tent, and had considered it sumptuous. Now another one, immense, lined with two layers of red and yellow material to ward off the heat and blinding light, was pitched in the centre of the camp. Another one, bigger still, quite black, of transparent goat's hair, was being set up further off and decorated with fringes of tufts of many-coloured wools, that looked festive in the breeze. This tent was to become the womens' domain; they kept there all the stores. Stacked in a line, these bags formed an improvised wall, covered by a long, beautifully designed carpet of the 'Gelim' type in scarlet and yellow geometrical patterns, that had been specially made for this purpose. It was in this tent that feasts were prepared, organised by the ladies who, however, disappeared behind a woven partition before the guests' arrival.

At these parties I was the only woman. I had visited the kitchen and watched the cook and his aides prepare the enormous quantities of rice, the 'kebab' and 'pilaw', the delicious stews, while, nearby, women were pounding herbs and grain, rhythmically and with traditional gestures.

Nasser Khan, followed by all his guests, entered the tent as soon as the servants had carried in the dishes. Balancing on their heads those big round trays, they had had to walk right through the camp. My place was laid between the Chief and his brother; it was easy to recognise for, out of deference for our customs, I had been given a white napkin. The Kashkais had also noticed that I never passed a spring or brook without kneeling beside it, plunging my face in the cool water and quenching my everlasting thirst; so they always provided a mug of icy liquid, and kept it constantly filled. Apparently, the Kashkais do not drink during meals, and are satisfied with their numerous glasses of tea.

Even when they are giving a party, the Kashkai eat quickly, picking from the various dishes the food that strikes their fancy, and mixing rice, meat, vegetables; instead of sauce, they add a spoonful or two of sour milk: it gives the food an unexpected and excellent flavour. I also found out, parched as I was by the dry wind and burning sun, that sour milk, mixed with water – 'dukh' the national drink – is pleasant and refreshing. For dessert we were served dates, stewed fruit and some excellent preserves.

It was in this tent that I met Malek Mansur's wife: cured of her fever, she was organising our first banquet there, and supervising the servants who, having removed their canvas shoes – the rope-soled 'giveh' worn all over Persia – were setting the dishes on the carpet. Formerly, to protect these beautiful rugs, 'Kalamkar' were spread over them during meals and served as tablecloths. They must have been very pretty. Now, alas, a sheet of plastic is used for the same purpose; this is certainly convenient and easy to keep clean, but I regretted the more decorative, if less modern and practical, printed cloths.

I had caught glimpses of Malek Mansur's wife as she rode into camp: she wore a white tulle skirt falling to the ground, and was covered back and front by another garment – a kind of scapulary made of material of vivid violet colour, contrasting with the green velvet bodice and the blue kerchief that hid the long plaits of her hair. All these colours looked most delightful as the lady moved in the sombre tent, walking with a rolling of the hips that swished her skirts about.*

We could not speak to each other, but she smiled at me in a frank and charming way. She seemed shy and did not care to be photographed, so I did not insist. In my film, though I would have liked to take many pictures of her, she is only seen from time to time and in the distance, flitting from tent to tent. She is herself the owner of vast territories situated beyond the range of mountains. But she seldom leaves this rough, hard life, sharing as she does the tastes of her husband.

The Il Khan's young sister, Molki, whom I had also met, told me about her sister-in-law's wedding. This ceremony is the occasion of festivities and rejoicings. Invitations are sent out by riders; friends and neighbours assemble bringing gifts, usually a lamb whose wool has been dyed a vivid colour. All the guests bring wood; this is indispensable in a country where fuel is scarce. A large supply will be needed, not only to prepare the food, but chiefly to build on top

---

* The tunique is called 'Piran'. The short-waisted, tight-fitting jacket, 'arkhalogh', has very long sleeves, slit at the wrists and covering the hands, and is made often of velvet or brocade. The hair is covered by a veil of light, transparent material: gauze or embroidered tulle, the 'charghad' held in place by a silk scarf, the 'kalaghi'. This scarf, wound around the head, is sometimes used to protect the face from sun or dust, and is then worn over a sun-shield made of horse-hair, the 'pitchè'.

of a high stone cairn a huge bonfire around which the women and girls dance. With hieratic gestures, girls of the Amalè Tribe will pound the rice and prepare it for the feast. These gatherings last from at least three days to two weeks. For Malek Mansur's wedding they actually lasted three full weeks!

As they ended, a cavalcade of three thousand rode out to fetch the waiting bride. Like Bibi Khanum, she is of the neighbouring Kashkuli Tribe, famed for its women and their beauty. She mounted a white horse and was led three times around the family hearth, then rode towards her future husband's camp, while horsemen galloped about her. According to Kashkai custom, the bride does not ride alone: she shares her horse with a young boy who sits behind her; his presence is thought to ensure that the first child shall be a son. As she approached the groom's tent, especially decorated for the occasion with rugs and blankets, and the symbols of light and happiness – a bowl of water and a mirror – her husband stepped out to meet her.

There are other feasts and festive occasions: great rejoicings take place for the birth of a son, and the ceremony of circumcision. Families and friends gather also for the funeral of parents and relatives. The women do not wail, as is customary in the East; instead, they sing a sad dirge. Mourning is worn; black clothes and black veil.

Women play an active part in tribal life. They are treated with great respect; their advice is listened to. One of their tasks is to supervise the transport and distribution of supplies during the migration. They go about freely, riding with the men. They do not wear a 'chador', but only occasionally veil themselves as a protection against the dust of the trail.

The camp was now pitched at the foot of the 'Black Mountain', of the Dinar range. In front of us the undulating, green and flower-decked Khosrow-Shirin plateau, empty and deserted in the morning, was now covered with a mass of flocks. The horses, in their new found freedom, frolicked and rolled over in the long grass.

As I returned from a long and solitary walk that took me to visit some humble tents in the foothills, I was invited to join Malek Mansur and his friends who, all afternoon, had been discussing political events. I was asked to taste one of the Tribe's delicacies – grape-flavoured sherbet. I was astonished, for where could one find

ice at that hour and on the burning plain? On top of the mountains
the spring snows had not yet melted. Men and mules had been sent
up; the snow, packed into bundles of sweet smelling herbs, and
covered by sacking, was brought to us. In a corner of the tent, the
servant who usually prepared tea was busy with an American
machine; turning the handle, he crushed the snow into thin flakes
and mixed them with the juice of over-ripe grapes, sweetened by
the Shiraz sun. In the heat, in the shade of the tent, this was the
most exquisite drink. Malek Mansur told me that it had strengthen-
ing qualities; mountaineers always drink it before undertaking a
stiff climb. This is not astonishing: for in the Alps we sustain ourselves with doses of grape sugar. Fruit of the vine, snow of the hills,
flavoured with mountain perfumes – could any drink be more
perfect under those relentless skies?

Nasser Khan told me that his men do not shun stronger beverages.
When I arrived, I had been offered some occidental drinks. As I
had refused, every one out of courtesy had done the same. Faithful
Muslims, Shi'ite, the Kashkai are not, however, very strict observers
of the Mohammedan rites. Their nomadic life exempts them from
submitting to the Mullahs' influence, and while on the march they
cannot attend services in the mosques or be called regularly to prayer.
In these vast expanses I could see them, simply and without any
ostentation, alone or in small groups, kneel and bow towards Mecca.
At grips with an often hard, inclement climate, migrating on difficult
trails, they remain deeply religious, but are exempted from certain
rules. When, on the first day of Ramadan, I remarked that this
severe fast was not observed, Nasser Khan said that it would have
been different had they been in their homes in Firuzabad or Shiraz;
but, on the march or in camp, they were free to eat at will.

The sun set behind the hills. Like an antique frieze, a line of
camels, diminutive yet stately in the distance, was outlined against
the molten sky. The flocks had come and gone, the grass lay trodden,
and the scent of crushed herbs hung acrid on the still air.

In the black tent, emptied of its visitors, the soil was broken and
a fire built in this small pit. Around it the women, dressed in their
beautiful clothes, sat gazing at the dancing flames. Then one by one
they left, and once more, for the last time, Nasser Khan, his brother,
and all their young companions who were now my friends, came

and talked with me. The flames shot up, light and shadow played on the transparent dark tent; the rich tones of the beautiful 'Gelim' carpet; the screen of woven reeds.

I knew that, in all probability, I would never see Nasser Khan again. In the morning I would be off once more, across the desert, towards Isfahan, then farther still. Soon I would see our grey and clouded skies, early morning mist, traffic and noisy towns, crowded villages, smoking chimneys, factories . . . Knowing the drive to be long, on the morrow we would say a brief farewell. So that evening, the last minutes were precious.

In those few days I had listened to the Il Khan's dispassionate reasoning, contrasting so greatly with the excited and vapid discourses we sometimes have to put up with in these troubled times. I had learnt to recognise his sound judgement, his fairness, his respect for tradition and family life, his patient attention to all problems, his constant care for the migrating multitudes. His moral stamina marked him as the leader.

When his name was mentioned, humble people nodded smilingly, severe and austere features lit up; for greater than his intelligence and power are his understanding and love for his Tribes.

KHOSROW-SHIRIN, *May* 1953
CRANS-SUR-SIERRE, *July-August* 1954

Appendix I

A BRIEF SURVEY OF THE PRINCIPAL TRIBES OF IRAN

FROM time immemorial, nomads have invaded Iran and led their herds and flocks on moors and hills of the plateau; prevented often from settling there by the influx of other hordes. Moving down from Central Asia, time and time again they have swept over the land in their eternal quest for pastures. What made them leave steppes and highlands, to start off on adventurous treks? Were they abandoning their familiar surroundings, forced by prolonged drought or some calamity? Were they tempted by tales of fabulous riches, and the hopes of finding lusher grass and more fertile plains? Were they forsaking their ancestral haunts, their numbers having become too great for the land to support them?

Or were they hounded out of their territories by neighbouring and envious tribes whose power was growing?

Or was it, for these hordes accustomed to rough life, to constant fights with inclement and hard climates, just the lust of battle and the intoxicating joy of plunder?

Nobody knows if the Aryans, the 'Ancestors' or 'Nobles', whose origin is mysterious, and whose name, Iran, was given to Persia, penetrated into the country through the Caucasus or the Turkestan. When the Huns began their long trek towards Europe, other nomads became powerful in Mongolia. These regions belonged to the boldest. Their inhabitants were called the 'Strong', the 'Turks'. Centuries later, leaving the Altaï Mountains, the wind-swept plains they marched over Turan and Asia Minor.

When the Mongols swept over the land, burning and plundering in their turn, they were not less cruel, and built themselves towers of skulls as triumphal monuments to their victories. Fought off in turn by the reigning monarchs, they eventually receded to the limits of the empire. Some disappeared altogether. Others changed from raging warriors to pacific shepherds and settled to a nomadic or semi-nomadic life, finding in the highlands of the Persian plateau a resemblance to their former lands. These repeated invasions have altered Iran's original population.

The nomads, living side-by-side with the peasants, despised these 'yellow faces' and, considered themselves the 'Lords of the Mountains'. In years of famine, they would swoop down upon the villages and fertile plains, killing and plundering as they went.

The tribes of Persia are now confined to definite territories. The most important of them are these:

In the east, near India, the BALUCH have settled to a sedentary life. They originally came from the Caspian Sea, emigrated towards Kerman, and reached the shores of the Gulf of Oman. They are, for the greater part, in Baluchistan; only a few live in Persia. Generally peaceful peasants, they speak an Iranian dialect. They are Sunnite, though subject to Shi'ite influence.

The HAZARÈ are on the border of Afghanistan, and mostly in that country: they infiltrate however into Persia because the soil there is more fertile. They are Shi'ite, speak Persian, but are in reality Mongol. They are peaceful.

The TURCOMAN are a warrior tribe of Central Asia; they live in the great Turkmen plain, their centre being Gurgan. They have always swept down over north-eastern Persia in plundering raids, and have been constantly fought by the Shahs. Established mostly in Russia, they were mobile, moving easily over the border after raids, leaving terror behind them. Their area even now is considered unsafe. The Turcoman speak Turkish, and have, like the Kurd, their own literature. They are not considered handsome, but have flat features, rendered picturesque by round fur hats.

The SHAH-SAWA, or 'followers of the Shah', live on the west coast of the Caspian, near Ardèbil, close to the Russian border. They were deported to the neighbourhood of lake Urmiyè in the 1880's, but returned to their former regions. The closing of the Russian frontier has forced them to become sedentary, but they still love their fire-arms and their horses.

Another group of SHAH-SAWA lives close to Teheran.

The GHASSEMABAD live on the south Caspian shores, not far from Ramsar. They came from the Caucasus and settled in the days of Shah Abbas. They are very different from the local inhabitants of the Guilan province: tall and slim. The women wear flounced skirts; the men tight-fitting trousers and short jackets.

The KURD are one of the oldest tribes of Iran, already mentioned under the name of 'CARDUQUES' by Xenophon. They opposed Alexander the Great. Later, they were submerged by the Arab conquest. When the Safawide Shahs waged war against the Ottoman Sultans, the Kurd seized this occasion to regain an independant existence. They organised a sort of feudal system, grouping themselves under the authority of a chieftain who dwelt in a fortified castle with his warriors, protecting the peasants and the shepherds.

They have been subjected to Russian influence since the beginning of the nineteenth century. Incapable of a united effort, fighting among themselves, they have always, however, hoped to form an independent state. Dominated by the Turks, they joined forces with the Ottomans and massacred the Christian Armenians, to be, in their turn, decimated by the Turks.

PLATE 31   'I had visited the kitchen and watched the cook and his aides'
(Page 105)

PLATE 32   'As I returned from a walk that took me to visit
some humble tents.' A Kashkai family (Page 107)

In 1919, at the Peace Conference, Sharif Pasha tried to create 'Great Kurdistan', but this State only existed on paper. Mustapha Kemal, who wanted to form a homogeneous nation, did away with the remaining principalities. In 1937, they were massacred and their villages bombed. Approximately 1,500,000 are settled in Iran; 496,000 in Iraq; a smaller group of about 25,000 lives in Syria, others in Turkey.

From their past feudal system they have kept the clan formation, the need to break up into small groups that quarrel continuously among each other.

The Kurd are semi-nomadic, living in villages during part of the year – from five to eight months. When the harvest is in, they lead their flocks to well-defined pasture lands. The men wear big turbans, ornamented with hanging tassels, a coloured shirt and a large sash often made of silk. Their trousers are narrow-legged, puffing out from the knees up. They wear the thick-soled canvas 'guiveh' shoes. Their women are independent, have influence in the affairs of the clan and have been known even to become chiefs of the tribes.

At their origin they were ill-defined pagans. After the Arab conquest they became Sunnite for the greater part. Some, however, have remained faithful to the Yezidi religion of 'devil worshippers'.

The LUR live in Luristan, and comprise four groups of tribes: the Lur proper; the Kuhgilui; the Mamasani and the Bakhtiyari.

Their greatest ambition is to be armed with a gun and cartridges. They were troublesone amd resisted to the utmost Riza Shah Pahlevi's plans to disarm and pacify them. Had they been united, they might have succeeded. They do not obey a chief, but live in a state of anarchy. They are notorious for their banditry. Travelling in their country in 1931, Freya Stark could write: 'This is a thoroughly risky country. A bullet may meet one around any corner . . . "Are there any police?" asked Hadji, . . . "There were two; they have been shot," said Keram carelessly . . .'

Big and strong, courageous to foolhardiness, the Lur live on a land that is extremely fertile, from the produce of their flock, and, when possible, from plunder.

The KUHGILUI are about 40,000 and are friendly towards the Kashkai.

The Mamasani live in the south, near Bebehan. One of the tribes composing this group is famous for its courage and ferocity. The warriors bare their chests in battle, as if to offer themselves to a swifter death; in fact, they have realised that a wound is not so dangerous if the dirt of a more or less filthy garment cannot penetrate it. Remarkable shots and horsemen, the Mamasani were feared by their neighbours and by the Iranian army; they lived for war and preferred plunder to work.

The Bakhtiyari are one of the most powerful tribes. They played an active part in forcing Shah Mohammed Ali to abdicate in 1909, when they marched on

H

Teheran. The petrol concessions of the Anglo Iranian Oil Company are on their lands, and the chiefs and the tribes receive shares in this company. They were very friendly towards the English. Riza Shah Pahlevi sought to destroy them, and they have never regained their former strength and influence. They are still about 200,000, but weakened by the Shah. Inveterate opium smokers, they seem to have lost their energy. Their music, which is remarkable, influenced and inspired Borodin.

The ARAB. Between the Luristan Mountains and the Persian Gulf are some Arab tribes, governed by Sheikhs who are big landownders.

The KHAMSÈ, as indicated by their name, are composed of five groups: three Arab groups and two Turkish who, to resist Kashkai influence, decided to choose a common chief in the Kawam family of Shiraz; but they are ruled now by a military officer appointed by the Governor of Shiraz. These groups are: the Arab, the Basiri, the Ainalu, the Baharlu and the Nafar. They number about 70,000. The first two are of Arab race and speak an arabic and Persian dialect; the Ainalu and Baharlu speak Turkish and the Nafar a mixture of Turkish. They occupy an area east and south west of the Kashkai, with whom they are not on good terms.

The Arabs entered Fars shortly after the Arab conquest in the seventh century. They are nomads at heart and resumed their nomadic life after Riza Shah Pahlevi's abdication. Those who are settled are bad cultivators and live poorly. These nomads hire their mules and camels for transport. They are good weavers of rugs and produce a large part of the Fars carpets.

The Basiri are a mixture of Arab and Persian, and claim to have entered Fars through Khorasan. They are the richest of this group.

The Ainalu emigrated into Fars from Turkestan in the eighteenth century. They are reputed to be honest and reliable.

The Baharlu came to Fars in the twelfth and thirteenth centuries and are of Turkish origin. Though they were once fierce fighters, they are now settled and are losing their spirit of independence and their strength.

The Nafar are a mixture of Turkish races. They live in a hot and barren country.

The KASHKAI speak a Turkish dialect. In the 1914 war they sided with the Germans under the influence of Wassmuss, the German Lawrence. Despoiled by Riza Shah Pahlevi, they have regained their strength.

During the 1945 revolt of the tribes, the Kashkai played a great part. Their chief, Nasser Khan, whose power is important in southern Iran, used his influence in opposing Communism and the Tudeh Party.

The frontiers of Kashkai territory are:
    to the west: Khuzistan
    to the north and north-east: the neighbourhood of Isfahan
    to the south-east: the neighbourhood of Bander Abbas

to the south-west: close to the Persian Gulf of which they are separated by the Makran Range.

The Kashkai, I was repeatedly told, are one of the most important tribes of Iran; they are also the most advanced, and one of the richest.

Accounts of their origin differ. Some say that they lived in Turan, in the days of Jengis Khan, and were brought to Iran by Nadir Shah; they first lived in Khalajistan, then most of them settled in Fars. Because of their name, others think that they came from Kashgar in the wake of Hulagu. Others again, and this seems to be the most commonly accepted version, presume them to be of Turkish race; their dialect is common to southern Turkey and is spoken in Azerbaijan and the northern Caucasus. The Kashkai claim to be of the white race, of which they have the characteristics, and of Aryan descent.

It is difficult to be sure. The Khalaj Tribes, for instance, are one of the twenty-two Tribes of the Turkish 'Ghuzz'. They came to Fars through Khala-jistan, a district near Savè, west of Kumm. The inhabitants of the villages in this region speak a Turkish dialect, and are a mixture of Khalaj and Bayat. The Khalaj now are extinct, though a small Bayat clan still exists. The Kashkai only became united in the eighteenth century, under the rule of Jani Agha, the first Il Khan, and the Khalaj joined up with them in the nineteenth century.

Could each one of these four versions contain a fragment of truth? If the Khalaj accepted the Il Khan's authority at so late a date, would it not have been possible for the other clans and tribes, though coming from different regions, to unite in the course of the centuries?

These different beliefs show that the Kashkai, like other nomad tribes, are not a fixed, immutable entity, but subject to changes and fluctuations. At one time they may think it in their interest to join forces, to unite under an elected Chief. He is not necessarily chosen among the clans themselves. The tribes, and this goes for all of them, have been known at times to prefer the authority of some local lord, or a member of some influential family. If the Chief is strong and his administration well organised, the tribes will prosper. If not, they are liable to disband, and seek their fortunes elsewhere. Should the Chief die, or be defeated in battle, some of his partisans may straggle away, eventually joining forces with more powerful neighbours, or even with their former foes.

The Kashkai are nomads; during eight months of the year they live under tents, shepherding their flocks. But they also cultivate the soil: in winter, in the warm climate of the south, during summer, in the high but fertile valleys of the Semiran region. Their crops are varied, they produce wheat and cereals in abundance and of excellent quality. The Kashkai are first and foremost breeders. Their flocks of sheep are their fortune, and enable them to make their celebrated rugs. Their breeds of horses are famous.

They migrate over territory that lies close to the Persian Gulf. Oil is found there and constitutes one of the land's reserves. In April, leaving the lower coun-try, averaging 2,000 feet where the heat becomes extreme, they move by stages, past Shiraz, to their summer grazing-grounds, south west of Isfahan. These are situated at a height of from 6,000 to 8,000 feet, the summits of these mountain ranges reaching from ten to twelve thousand feet. This is the largest annual migration of any Persian tribe. The Kashkai number approximately 400,000, and their flocks are estimated at 7,000,000 head.

Under powerful Khans, the Kashkai played an important part in Fars during the nineteenth century. In more recent years, Riza Shah Pahlevi's policy of forcibly settling the tribes, of weakening or dispersing them, caused them severe hardship and misery. They were prevented from migrating, the tracks they followed were cut by military patrols. Some were forced to spend the winter months in the high mountains and suffered greatly, their cattle and horses dying of cold. (The famed horse-breeders of the Darrèshuri tribe lost nearly all their horses.) Or else they were obliged to spend the summer in the warm and marshy regions. Accustomed to a free and roving life, to the cleanliness of ever-changing camp sites, the accumulated dirt around their houses, the smoke-filled huts, made them ill. The rate of disease increased rapidly.

Sawlat-al-Dawlè, the Il Khan was imprisoned together with other chieftains. When, in 1941, Riza Shah Pahlevi abdicated, the Kashkai forced the army to evacuate their lands. Nasser Khan, Sawlat-al-Dawlè's first born son, joined the tribes immediately; their leader ever since, he shares with them their nomadic existence.

Slowly, through the years, the tribes have rebuilt their herds.

In 1946, Olivier Garrod could write of them: 'The qualities which stand out clearest among the Kashkais are the high level of family life, strongly influenced by women; the well developed communal sense; the high degree of art whereby articles of daily use are made beautiful; the superb horses and horsemanship of the Darrèshuri; the way the Khans have clung to nomadic life and remained close to their people; and, lastly, the great prosperity of the tribe in comparison with that of the less fortunate neighbours . . . ensure that the Kashkais reach the highest level of nomadic civilisation.'

Appendix II

THE KASHKAI CLANS

(As indicated by Massoud Keyan and M. A. Jamalzadè)

DARRÈSHURI	5,000 families
	live at Ildernahri; Galèzan; Garm-Abad; Sèmiran (upper regions)
KASHKULI	3,000 families
	live near Ardekan, till the col of Vizak
SHESH BOLUKI	6,000 families
	live on the frontiers of Chafta-Donguè (As Pass; Kushk-é-zard; Kuh-è-Sefid; Namadan)

AMALÈ	3,000 families
FARSIMADAN	2,000 families
	their name means: 'who does not speak Persian'
	live at Pa Déna
SAFI-KHANÈ	800 families
	live at Khosrow-Shirin
IGDER	500 families
BOLUYÈ	
HASHEM KHANÈ	200 families
	live at Cherhan belong to the Amalè of the Il Khan
BOLUYÈ-HAJJI	
TAHMASP-KHANÉ	200 families
	live at Gare-Tappè; Khosrow-Shirin
CHAIBUTCHÈ	
AGHRI GALEZAN	600 families
	live at As Pass; Khosrow-Shirin
NAMADI GALEZAN	500 families
	live at Jadegan; Balayè; Semiran
NITCHAK GALEZAN	40 families
	(belong to the Amalè of the Il Khan)
GHAZALU GALEZAN	80 families
CHARBONICHÈ	
MALILVAND	
KARA KHANLU	300 familes
	live at Vanda; Karzani; Zanguenè; Lak
KOYONLU	200 families
	live with the Kashkuli
KARAK HANLU	
KALÈ SEFID	
BAYAT SAT-ALI	300 families
	live at Khan Khowiss (19 miles from Shiraz)
	150 families
	live at Bajgah
BAYAT SHAHVARDI	100 families
RAHINI	300–600 families
	live 8 miles from Hana. One group lives near Yezdikh-wast
NOKHANLU	80 families
	live near the river Rahini
SAKHAZ	40 families
	belong to the Amalè of the Il Khan; a part of them live with the Kashkuli
AURYAD	150 families
	belong to the Amalè of the Il Khan.

AGHBEHI	200 families
KARABEHI	80 families
	live near Darekord
YALMÈ SARFARAZ	300 families
	live in the neighbourhood of Huneghan and Karruyè
YALMÈ ABDUL-KHANI	50 families
JORKANI	200 families
	live at Sèdè; Khosrow-Shirin
JORKANI ITAM	40 families
	live at Beiza
BOLHASANI	30 families
	live at Mozun; Kazerun
BOHLULI	
KARA BEGH	50 families
	belong to the Amalè of the Il Khan
BOHLULI	
HAJJI FATH-ALI	60 families
	live at Jerrè; Faniur
ASLANI	80 families
	live at Garmabad
KHARATCHÈ	400 families
	live at Badna

etc. etc.

The Il Khan is of the Shahlu tribe. This tribe only comprises four or five families.

The tribes and sub-tribes of the Kashkai numbered forty-four at their origin and are now fifty-five.

These tribes are all nomadic or semi-nomadic; some have a tendency to settle.

The KASHKULI represent 'nomadic life at its highest'. The SHESH BOLUKI are the largest and the wealthiest. Their rugs and those of the KASHKULI are among the finest. The DARRÈSHURI are the most famous horse-breeders.

It is difficult to state the exact number of Kashkai. The tribes' custom is to count in terms of 'Families', 'houses' or 'Tents'.

The Kashkai name has been written in different ways: Kashka'i, Gashghai, Quashqu'ai.

Nasser Khan and his family have quite recently decided to adopt the simpler spelling of 'GASHGAI'.

BIBLIOGRAPHY

ABBOTT, K. E. 'Notes on a Journey eastwards from Shiraz to Fessa and Darab, thence westwards by Jehrum to Kazerun, in 1850.' *Journal of the Royal Geographical Society*; Vol. XXVII, March 1857.

Ame de l'Iran (L'). Articles by R. Grousset; H. Massé; L. Massignon; A. Godard; Y. Godard; etc. Paris, 1951.

ANDREAS, F. C. *Six Months in Persia.*

ARBERRY, A. J. *Sufism.* Allen & Unwin, London, 1950.

—— *The Holy Koran.* Allen & Unwin, London, 1953.

Art en Mésopotamie (L'). 'Cahiers d'Art.' Paris, 1935.

Athar-è-Iran. Annales du Service Archéologique de l'Iran. Paul Geuthner, Paris, 1936, 1937, 1938, 1949.

AUBIN, E. *La Perse d'Aujourd'hui, Iran, Mésopotamie.* Paris, 1901.

BAZIN, G. *Histoire de l'Art.* Paris, 1953.

BELL, GERTRUDE L. *Letters.* Ernest Benn, London, 1927.

BINYON, R., WILKINSON, J. V. S., and GRAY, B. *Persian Miniature Painting.* Oxford University Press, 1933.

BRADLEY-BIRT, F. B. *Through Persia from the Gulf to Ararat.* Murray, 1909.

BROWNE, E. G. *A Literary History of Persia.* 4 Vol. Cambridge University Press, 1928. (Reprinted, 1951.)

—— *A Year amongst the Persians.* 1893. (New edition: Cambridge University Press, 1926.)

CAMERON, G. *History of Early Iran.* Chicago, 1936.

CERAM, C. W. *Gods, Graves and Scholars.* Gollancz, London, 1952.

CHAMPDER, A. *Cyrus.* Albin Michel, Paris, 1952.

CHARDIN. *Voyages du Chevalier Chardin en Perse et Autres Lieux de l'Orient.* Langlès. 10 Vol. Paris, 1811.

CHRISTENSEN, A. *L'Iran sous les Sassanides.* Ejnar Munksgaard, Copenhagen, 1936.

Civilisation Iranienne (La). Payot. Paris, 1952.

PREMIERES CIVILISATIONS (LES). Presses Universitaires de France. Paris, 1950.

CLAVIJO, RUY GONCALEZ DE. *Embassy to Tamerlane.* Routledge, London, 1928.

CONTENAU, G. *Manuel d'Archéologie Orientale.* Vol. I. Paris, 1927; Vols. II and III, Paris, 1931; Vol. IV, Paris, 1947.

—— *Les Antiquités Orientales.* Vol. I, Paris, 1927; Vol. II, Paris, 1930.

—— *La Civilisation d'Assur et de Babylone.* Paris, 1948.

—— *La Civilisation des Hittites.* Payot, Paris, 1948.

CUMONT, F. *Les Religions Orientales dans le Paganisme Romain*. Paul Geuthner, Paris, 1929.

CURZON, G. N. *Persia and the Persian Question*. 2 Vol. 1892.

DELAPORTE, L. 'L'Art de l'Asie Antérieure', in *Nouvelle Historie Universelle de l'Art*. Paris, 1932.

—— *Les Hittites*. Paris, 1936.

—— *Le Proche-Orient Asiatique*. Paris, 1948.

DARMESTETER, J. *Coup d'Oeil sur l'Histoire de la Perse*. Paris, 1885.

—— *Les Origines de la Poèsie Persane*. Paris, 1885.

DEMORGNY, G. 'Les Réformes Administratives en Perse'; 'Les Tribus du Fars'; in *Revue du Monde Musulman*. Paris, 1913.

DIEULAFOY, M. *L'Art Antique de la Perse*. Paris, 1884-1885.

EDWARDS, A. C. *The Persian Carpet*. Duckworth, London, 1953.

Encyclopedie de l'Islam. 5 Vol.

FIRDAWSI. *Le Livre des Rois*. Translated by J. Mohl. 7 Vol. Paris, 1876.

FRANKFORT, H. *Cylinder-Seals*. Macmillan, London, 1939.

FORBES, J. *Metallurgy in Antiquity*. Leyden, 1950.

FOUCHER, A. 'Les grandes Voies de Communication de l'Extrême-Orient à la Méditerranee à travers l'Iran', in *La Civilisation Iranienne*. Payot. Paris, 1952.

GARROD, O. 'The Qashqai Tribe of Fars', in *Journal of the Royal Central Asian Society*. 1946.

GOBINEAU, A. DE. *Trois Ans en Asie*. 2 Vol. Paris, 1922.

—— *Les Religions et les Philosophies dans l'Asie Centrale*. 2 Vol. Paris. 1923.

GODARD, A. *Les Bronzes du Luristan*. van Oest, Paris, 1931.

—— 'L'Art de la Perse Ancienne', in *Nouvelle Histoire Universelle de l'Art*. Paris, 1932.

—— *Athar-è-Iran*. Annales du Service Archéologique de l'Itan. Teheran, 1936, 1937, 1938, 1949.

—— *Le Trésor de Ziwiyè*. Paris, 1950.

—— 'Table Chronologique des Dynasties de l'Iran', in *France Libre*, No. 9, Teheran, 1943.

GODARD, Y. 'L'Aventureux Art Scythe', in *L'Ame de l'Iran*. Albin Michel, Paris, 1951.

—— *Athar-è-Iran*.

—— 'Les Capitales de l'Iran', in *France Libre*, No. 9. Teheran, 1943.

GROUSSET, R. *Sur les Traces du Bouddha*. Plon, Paris, 1929.

—— *L'Epopée des Croisades*. Plon, Paris, 1939.

—— *Histoire des Croisades*. 3 Vol. Paris, 1934-1935.

—— *Le Conquérant du Monde*. Albin Michel, Paris, 1944.

—— *Bilan de l'Histoire*. Paris, 1946.

—— *L'Empire des Steppes*. Paris, 1948.

HAFIZ. *Ghazels de Hafiz.* Translated by A. Guy. Paul Geuthner, Paris, 1927.

HERODITUS. Histories. Dent, London.

HERZFELD, E. *Archaeological History of Iran.* London, 1935.

—— *Iran in the Ancient East.* New York, 1941.

HEYD, W. *Histoire du Commerce du Levant au Moyen-Age.* Translated by Furcy Raynaud. Leipsig, 1923.

HOUSSAY, F. 'Etudes sur la Perse Méridionale. La Structure du Sol et son Influence sur la Vie des Habitants', in *Annales de Géographie*, III, 1894.

HOUTUM-SCHINDLER, A. *Eastern Persian Irak.* London, 1897.

HOWORTH, H. H. *History of the Mongols.* Vol. III: The Mongols of Persia. London, 1888. Vol. IV: Supplement and Index. Longmans, London, 1927.

HROZNY, B. *Histoire de l'Asie Antérieure.* Translated by M. David. Payot, Paris, 1947.

HUXLEY, J. *From an Antique Land.* Parrish, London, 1954.

HUART, C., and DELAPORTE, L. *L'Iran Antique dans la Civilisation Iranienne.* Paris, 1943.

JAMALZADÈ, M. A. 'Apercus sur la Situation Sociale et Economique de l'Iran', in *Revue Internationale du Travail*, Vol. LXIII, No. 1, Jan. 1951, Geneva.

KEYHAN, MASSOUD. *La Géographie détaillée de l'Iran.* 3 Vol. Teheran, 1932.

KHANLARI, P. 'Hafiz de Shiraz', in *L'Ame de l'Iran.* Paris, 1951.

KÜHNEL, E. *Miniaturmalerei im Islamischen Orient.* Berlin, 1922.

LAYARD, E. H. *Early Adventures in Persia, Susiana and Babylonia.* 2 Vol. John Murray, London, 1887.

LAMB, HAROLD. *Genghis Khan.* Butterworth, London.

—— *Tamerlane: Earth Shaker.* Butterworth, London, 1928.

—— *Omar Khayyam.* Doubleday Doran, New York, 1934.

LESCOT, R. 'Quelques Ruba 'iyat de Djalal-el-Din Rumi', in *France Libre*, No. 9, Teheran, 1943.

LE STRANGE, G. *The Lands of the Eastern Caliphate.* Cambridge University Press, 1905.

LOCKHART, L. *Nadir Shah.* Luzac, London, 1938.

MACLEAN, H. W. *Eastern Approaches.* Cape, London, 1949.

MAILLART, E. *The Cruel Way.* Heinemann, London, 1947.

MASSÈ, H. *Anthologie Persane.* Payot, Paris, 1950.

Memoires de la Délégation Archéeolgique Francaise en Perse.

MINORSKY, V. *Les Facteurs Historiques de l'Histoire Iranienne.*

—— Articles on 'Luristan', 'Kurdistan', 'Azerbaijan', etc., in *Encyclopedie de l'Islam.*

MORET, A., and DAVY, G. *Des Clans aux Empires.* Paris, 1923.

MORGAN, G. DE. *Mission Scientifique en Perse.* Vols. I and II: Etudes Géographiques. Paris, 1894-1895.

—— *L'Humanité Préhistorique.* Paris, 1921.

—— *Manuel de Numismatique Orientale.* 2 Vol. Paris, 1923.

OLÉARIUS, A. *Relation du Voyage d'Adam Oléarius en Moscovie, Tartarie et Perse.* 2 Vol. Paris, 1866.

PARROT, A. *Découverte des Mondes Ensevelis.* Neuchâtel, Paris, 1952.

PERCHERON, M. *Les Conquérants d'Asie.* Payot, Paris, 1950.

PERROT, G., and CHIPIEZ, C. H. *Histoire de l'Art dans l'Antiquité.* 2 Vol. T.V: La Perse, Paris, 1890.

PÉZARD, M. *La Céramique Archaïque de l'Islam.* 2 Vol. Paris, 1920.

PIRENNE, J. *Civilisations Antiques.* Albin Michel, Paris, 1951.

POLO, MARCO. *The Travels of Marco Polo.* Dent, London, 1925.

PRAWDIN, M. *The Mongol Empire.* Allen & Unwin, London, 1953.

RADET, G. *Alexandre le Grand.* Paris, 1931.

REITLINGER, G. A. *Tower of Skulls.* Duckworth, London, 1932.

RUTTEN, M. *Arts et Styles du Moyen-Orient Ancien.* Larousse, Paris, 1950.

SAINT-PHALLE, A. DE. *D'Assurbanipal è Saint Paul.* Gallimard, Paris, 1951.

SARRE, F. *Die Kunst des Alten Persiens.* Berlin, 1923.

SARRE, F., and HERTZLEFD, E. *Iranische Felsreliefs.* Berlin, 1910.

SAWYER, H. A. 'The Bakhtiari Mountains and Upper Elam', in *Geographical Journal*, IV, 1894.

SCHMIDT, E. *Persepolis.* Vol. I. Chicago, 1953.

STACK, E. *Six Months in Persia.* 1882.

STAHL, A. F. 'Reisen in Nord und Zentral Persien', in *Pertermanns Mitteilungen*, 1895.

STARK, F. *The Valley of the Assassins.* Murray, London, 1934.

STEIN, A. 'An Archaeological Tour in the Ancient Persias', in *Irak*, Vol. III, 1936.

STOUCHINE, I. *La Peinture Iranienne sous les Derniers Abbasides et les Il-Khans.* Bruges, 1930.

SYKES, SIR PERCY. *A History of Persia.* Macmillan, London, 1930.

SYKES, C. *Wassmuss.* Longmans, London.

A Survey of Persian Art. 6 Vol. Oxford University Press, 1938-1939.

TAVERNIER, J. B. *Les Six Voyages de Jean Baptiste Tavernier en Turquie, en Perse, et aux Indes,* etc., 3 Vol. 1712.

VIEYRA, M. *Hittite Art.* Tiranti, London, 1955.

WILSON, SIR A. T. 'Notes on a Journey from Bandar Abbas to Shiraz, via Lar', in *Geographical Journal*, XXXI, 1908.

—— *The Persian Gulf.* London, 1928 (2nd Edition, 1954.)

XENOPHON. *The Persian Expedition.* Translated by R. Warner. Penguin Books, London, 1949.

ZERVOS, C. *L'Art de la Mésopotamie de la Fin du IVième. Millénaire au XVième Siècle avant notre Ere.* Ed. 'Cahiers d'Art'. Paris, 1935.

INDEX